THE AUSTRALIAN
Women's Weekly
home baked

Contents

For the wonderful aroma of home baking, you don't have to become an expert baker: build up a small stock of spices, sugars and essences in your store cupboard and with a little practice, you'll be able to magic up a batch of muffins, scones or spectacular cakes, with very little bother. Store your efforts in a tin and put one in a lunch box or share with friends – so simple and so rewarding!

Pamela Clark

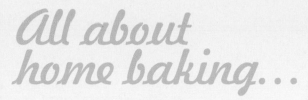

All about home baking...

Oven types and rack position

There are many different types of ovens and energy sources, so it is important that you get to know your oven – particularly when it comes to baking. The recipes in this book were tested in domestic-size electric ovens.

☞ If using a fan-assisted oven, check the operating instructions for best results. As a rule, reduce the baking temperature by 10°C to 20°C when using the fan during baking; cakes, biscuits and slices might also take slightly less time to bake than specified. Some ovens give better results if the fan is used for part of the baking time; it is usually best to introduce the fan about halfway through the baking time.

☞ None of the recipes in this book have been tested in a microwave or microwave/convection oven, as the baking time and result would be different from a conventionally baked cake, biscuit or slice.

☞ We positioned the oven racks and pan(s) so that the top of the baked cake will be roughly In the centre of the oven. If in doubt, check the manufacturer's instructions for your oven.

☞ Several items can be baked at the same time, either on the same or different racks, provided they do not touch each other, or the oven wall or door, to allow for an even circulation of heat.

☞ To ensure even browning, pans on different racks should exchange positions about halfway through baking time; move the lower pans to the top rack, and vice versa. This will not affect results if you do this carefully and quickly.

☞ Best results are obtained by baking in an oven preheated to the desired temperature; this takes about 10 minutes. This rule is particularly important for cakes, biscuits or slices baked in under 30 minutes.

Helpful hints

☞ We do not recommend mixing cakes, biscuits or slices in blenders or processors unless specified in individual recipes.

☞ Use an electric beater to mix cakes, and always have the ingredients at room temperature, particularly the butter. Melted or extremely soft butter will alter the texture of the baked product.

☞ When measuring liquids, always stand the marked measuring jug on a flat surface and check at eye level for accuracy.

☞ Spoon measurements should be levelled off with a knife or spatula. Be careful when measuring ingredients such as honey or treacle.

What went wrong...

Unfortunately, cakes don't always emerge from the oven looking just like our photographs. The following is a troubleshooters' guide to get you and your cakes back on track.

My butter cake wasn't perfect...

Sinks in centre after removal from oven This generally means that the cake is undercooked.

Sinks in centre while still baking If the mixture is forced to rise too quickly because the oven is too hot, it will sink in the centre.

Sugary crust Butter and sugar have not been creamed sufficiently.

White specks on top Undissolved sugar, or insufficient creaming. In a light butter cake, it is better to use caster sugar, which dissolves easily.

Excessive shrinking The oven being too hot has caused cake to overcook.

Crumbles when cut Mixture may have been creamed too much, or eggs added too quickly.

Sticks to pan Too much sugar or other sweetening in recipe. If a recipe contains honey or golden syrup, or if you're using a new pan, it's wise to line the evenly greased pan with greased baking parchment.

Rises and cracks in centre Cake tin too small or oven too hot. Most cakes baked in loaf or ring tins crack slightly due to the confined space.

Collar around top outside edge Cake baked at too high a temperature.

Pale on top, brown underneath and sides Too large a tin, or lining paper too high around sides of tin.

Colour streaks on top Insufficient mixing of ingredients, or bowl scrapings not mixed thoroughly into cake mixture in tin.

Uneven rising Oven shelf not straight, oven not level on floor, or mixture not spread evenly in tin.

Holes in baked cake Mixture not creamed sufficiently or oven too hot.

Crusty, overbrowned, uncooked in centre Cake baked too long or at too high a temperature. Cake tin too small, causing top to overcook while cake not cooked through completely.

My fruit cake wasn't perfect...

Fruit sinks to bottom Fruit washed, but not dried thoroughly; cake mixture too soft to support weight of the fruit (caused by over-creaming). Self-raising flour may have been used in recipe instead of plain flour. Fruit should be finely chopped so mixture can support it more easily.

Doughy in centre Cake baked in too cold an oven, or not long enough.

Burnt bottom Wrong oven position. Cake baked at too high a temperature, or incorrect lining of tins. Rich fruit cakes require protection during long, slow baking time. Cakes that are 22cm or smaller require three thicknesses of baking-parchment lining; larger cakes need one or two sheets of brown paper and three sheets of baking parchment.

Cracks on top Cake baked at too high a temperature.

Uneven on top Oven shelf or oven not level, or mixture not spread evenly in tin (use a wet spatula to level top of cake mixture).

Creamed mixture curdles Eggs and butter not at room temperature to begin with, or eggs not added quickly enough to creamed butter and sugar mixture, or eggs used are too large for mixture to absorb the excess liquid. If eggs used are larger than 60g in weight, omit one of the number shown in ingredients list, or add only the yolk of one of the eggs. Curdled creamed mixture could cause the finished cake to crumble when cut.

Sinks in middle Self-raising flour used, or too much bicarbonate of soda. (Usually only plain flour is used in rich fruit cake, but sometimes a small portion of self-raising flour is added). Cake may not have been baked properly. To test, push sharp-pointed knife through centre to base of pan; blade surface helps distinguish between uncooked mixture or fruit and cooked mixture. Test only after minimum specified baking time.

My sponge cake wasn't perfect...

Small white specks on top Undissolved sugar; sugar should be added gradually to beaten eggs and beaten until completely dissolved between additions.

Shrinks in oven Cake baked at too high a temperature or for too long.

Shrinks and wrinkles during cooling Insufficient baking time, or cooling the cake in a draught.

Flat and tough Incorrect folding in of flour and liquid. Triple-sifted flour should be folded into mixture in a gentle, circular motion.

Pale and sticky on top Baking at too low an oven temperature, or wrong oven position.

Crusty Baking at too high an oven temperature, wrong oven position or tin too small. Using high-sided cake tins protects the cake mixture.

Sinks in centre Tin too small, causing cake to rise quickly, then fall in the centre.

Streaks on top Scrapings from mixing bowl not mixed into sponge mixture; scrapings are always slightly darker than the full amount of mixture.

Sponge rises too quickly Oven temperature is too high.

Sponge is undercooked Oven door may have been opened during first half of baking.

To test if cake is cooked

All baking times are approximate. Check your cake just after the suggested cooking time; it should be browned and starting to shrink from the sides of the tin. Feel the top with your fingertips; it should feel firm. You may want to insert a thin skewer in the deepest part of the cake (we prefer to use a metal skewer rather than a wooden one because any mixture that adheres to it is easier to see). Gently remove the skewer; it shouldn't have any uncooked mixture clinging to it. Do not confuse cake mixture with stickiness from fruit.

Getting it right...

Rubbing butter into flour

Using your fingers, lightly rub cold butter into the flour, lifting it up high and letting it fall back down into the bowl. This incorporates air, which is what makes pastry light. The process should be done fairly quickly. Rub just long enough to make the mixture crumbly with just a few odd lumps here and there – it should resemble breadcrumbs.

Separating egg whites

When separating egg yolk from the white, the egg has to be as fresh as possible. Crack the egg around the middle and, using both hands, break it into two halves, one in each hand. Tip the yolk back and forth from one shell to the other, letting the white trickle into a bowl while keeping the yolk in the shell. Be careful when doing this, because if one speck of yolk gets into the white, it won't be suitable for whisking.

Beating egg whites with an electric mixer

When beating egg whites, you are actually incorporating air, which increases the volume. First beat on a slow speed until everything has become bubbly, then increase the speed and continue beating until soft peaks form. Do not overbeat, as the whites will become dry and separate. The tiniest trace of yolk in the white means the white won't whisk; it is also important that the bowl and beaters are grease-free.

Levelling off flour in a measuring cup

Lightly spoon flour into the measuring cup, adding enough flour so it forms a dome over the top of the cup. Gently shake the cup. Use the back edge of a knife to level the flour by running it along the rim of the cup to remove the excess flour. Never measure ingredients over the mixing bowl containing other ingredients as you may accidentally tip the excess into the mixture, and this could ruin the whole recipe.

Preparing a cake tin

We use aluminium cake tins because they give the best results. Cake tins made from materials with various coatings, such as non-stick, work well provided that the surface is unscratched. Tins made from tin and stainless steel do not conduct heat as evenly as aluminium does.
To grease a cake tin, use either a light, even coating of cooking-oil spray, or a pastry brush to brush melted butter or margarine evenly over the base and sides.
Sometimes recipes call for a greased and floured cake tin. Simply grease the tin evenly (melted butter is best) and allow it to 'set' a minute or two before sprinkling a little flour evenly over the greased area.
Tap the tin several times on your bench then tip out the excess flour. To line a cake tin with baking parchment, trace around the base of the tin with a pencil onto baking parchment; cut out the shape slightly inside the pencil mark, so the paper fits snugly inside the greased tin. It is not necessary to grease the baking parchment once it is in position.

As a guide, cakes requiring 1 hour or longer to bake should have a baking parchment 'collar' extending about 5cm above the edge of the tin, to protect the top of the cake. The following method of lining round or square cake tins allows for this, using baking parchment:

☞ For sides, cut three paper strips long enough to fit around inside of the tin and 8cm wider than the depth of the tin. Fold strips lengthways about 2cm from the edge and make short diagonal cuts about 2cm apart, up to the fold. This helps ease the paper around the curves or corners of the tin, with the cut section fitting around the base.

☞ Using the base of tin as a guide, cut three paper circles (or squares) as instructed previously; position in base of tin after lining sides.

Cooling a cake

We have suggested standing times for cakes before turning onto wire racks to cool further. The best way to do this, after standing time has elapsed, is to hold the cake tin firmly and shake it gently, thus loosening the cake from the tin. Turn the cake, upside down, onto a wire rack, then turn the cake top-side up immediately using a second rack (unless directed otherwise). Some wire racks mark the cakes, particularly soft cakes such as sponges. To prevent this, cover the rack with baking parchment. Unless otherwise stated, all cakes (and slices) should be cooled to room temperature before icing or filling.

Storing cakes

Make sure your cake is at room temperature before storing it in an airtight container as close in size to the cake as possible; this minimises the amount of air around the cake. For those cakes that are suitable to freeze, it is usually better to freeze them unfilled and uniced because icing often cracks during the thawing process. Wrap or seal cakes in freezer bags, expelling as much air as possible. Cakes thaw best overnight in the refrigerator. Unfilled and uniced cakes can be frozen for up to three months.

Working with chocolate

Making white chocolate ganache

Ganache is a French term referring to a smooth mixture of cream and chocolate, although butter may sometimes be added. Boiled cream is poured over chopped chocolate and the mixture is stirred until velvety smooth. Stand mixture until desired consistency is reached. Different flavours, such as liqueurs and extracts, also can be added.

Making chocolate curls or flakes

Run a sharp vegetable peeler down the side of a large block of chocolate to create flakes. For curls, slightly soften the chocolate first, then drag a vegetable peeler down the side of the chocolate in one continuous movement. The harder you press the thicker the curls will be. Let the curls fall onto a cold baking-paper-lined tray. or a cold plate. Refrigerate until ready to use.

Muffins

BERRY MUFFINS
straight from the oven

crusty
CHEESE MUFFINS

Chocolate muffins

GINGER DATE MUFFINS
with caramel sauce

MUFFINS ARE SIMPLE TO
MAKE AND DELICIOUS EATEN
HOT, WARM OR COLD, WITH
OR WITHOUT BUTTER

Basic muffins

2½ cups (375g) self-raising flour
90g butter, chopped
1 cup (220g) caster sugar
1¼ cups (310ml) buttermilk
1 egg, lightly beaten

1 Preheat oven to 200°C/180°C fan-assisted. Grease 12-hole (⅓-cup/80ml) muffin tray.
2 Sift flour into large bowl, rub in butter. Stir in sugar, buttermilk and egg. Do not over-mix; mixture should be lumpy.
3 Spoon mixture into prepared tray, bake muffins 20 minutes.

prep and cook time 30 minutes
makes 12

Variations

fruit & spice Sift 3 teaspoons mixed spice with the flour; add 1 cup (190g) mixed dried fruit with the sugar.

date & orange Substitute 1 cup (160g) wholemeal self-raising flour for 1 cup of the self-raising flour in basic muffin recipe. Add 1½ cups (240g) stoneless chopped dates and 3 teaspoons grated orange rind with the sugar.

choc chip & walnut Add ¾ cup (140g) chocolate chips and 1 cup (120g) chopped walnuts with the sugar.

IT IS IMPORTANT NOT TO OVERMIX THE MUFFIN MIXTURE; IT REQUIRES MINIMUM MIXING AND SHOULD LOOK COARSE AND LUMPY. MUFFINS ARE COOKED WHEN THEY ARE BROWNED, RISEN, FIRM TO TOUCH AND BEGINNING TO SHRINK FROM THE SIDES OF THE TIN. IF IN DOUBT, PUSH A METAL OR WOODEN SKEWER INTO A MUFFIN. WHEN WITHDRAWN, THE SKEWER SHOULD BE CLEAN AND FREE FROM MUFFIN MIXTURE.

Choc honeycomb muffins

2 cups (300g) self-raising flour
¼ cup (55g) caster sugar
1 cup (190g) white chocolate chips
100g chocolate-coated honeycomb bar, chopped
1 egg, lightly beaten
60g butter, melted
1 cup (250ml) buttermilk
¼ cup (60ml) honey
1 teaspoon vanilla essence

1   Preheat oven to 200°C/180°C fan-assisted. Grease 12-hole (⅓-cup/80ml) muffin tray.
2   Sift flour and sugar into large bowl, stir in chocolate chips and honeycomb, then remaining ingredients.
3   Spoon mixture into prepared tray. Bake muffins about 20 minutes.

prep and cook time 35 minutes
makes 12

Ginger date muffins with caramel sauce

1 cup (160g) pitted chopped dates
⅓ cup (80ml) water
¼ teaspoon bicarbonate of soda
2 cups (300g) self-raising flour
1 cup (150g) plain flour
2 teaspoons ground ginger
½ teaspoon mixed spice
1 cup (200g) firmly packed brown sugar
2 teaspoons grated orange rind
1 egg, lightly beaten
1¼ cups (310ml) milk
¼ cup (60ml) vegetable oil
caramel sauce
1 cup (200g) firmly packed brown sugar
1 cup (250ml) double cream
40g butter

1 Preheat oven to 200°C/180°C fan-assisted. Grease 12-hole (⅓-cup/80ml) muffin tray.
2 Combine dates and water in pan, bring to boil, remove from heat, add soda, stand 5 minutes.
3 Sift dry ingredients into large bowl, stir in date mixture and remaining ingredients.
4 Spoon mixture into prepared tray. Bake muffins about 20 minutes. Serve warm with caramel sauce.
caramel sauce Combine all ingredients in pan, stir over heat, without boiling, until sugar is dissolved, then simmer, without stirring, for about 3 minutes, or until thickened slightly.

prep and cook time 40 minutes
makes 12

Blueberry muffins

2 cups (300g) self-raising flour
¾ cup (150g) firmly packed brown sugar
1 cup (150g) fresh or frozen blueberries
1 egg, lightly beaten
¾ cup (180ml) buttermilk
½ cup (125ml) vegetable oil

1 Preheat oven to 200°C/180°C fan-assisted. Grease six-hole
(¾-cup/180ml) muffin tray.
2 Sift dry ingredients into large bowl, stir in remaining ingredients.
3 Spoon mixture into prepared tray. Bake muffins about 20 minutes.

prep and cook time 30 minutes
makes 6

Apricot buttermilk muffins

1½ cups (225g) roughly chopped dried apricots
¼ cup (60ml) brandy
3 cups (450g) self-raising flour
125g butter, chopped
½ cup (110g) caster sugar
2 eggs, lightly beaten
¾ cup (180ml) buttermilk
apricot butter
60g butter
1 cup (160g) icing sugar
1 tablespoon brandy

1 Preheat oven to 200°C/180°C fan-assisted. Grease 12-hole
(⅓ cup/80ml) muffin tray.
2 Combine apricots and brandy in bowl, stand 20 minutes. Process
apricot mixture until finely chopped, reserve ¼ cup of apricot mixture.
3 Sift flour into large bowl, rub in butter. Stir in sugar, apricot mixture,
eggs and buttermilk.
4 Spoon mixture into prepared tray. Bake muffins about 20 minutes.
Serve with apricot butter.
apricot butter Beat butter in small bowl with electric mixer until as
white as possible. Gradually beat in icing sugar, brandy and reserved
apricot mixture.

prep and cook time 35 minutes
makes 12

Mixed berry muffins

2¼ cups (335g) self-raising flour
1 cup (220g) caster sugar
1 teaspoon vanilla extract
2 eggs, beaten lightly
100g butter, melted
1 cup (250ml) milk
1 teaspoon grated lemon rind
200g fresh or frozen mixed berries

1   Preheat oven to 200°C/180°C fan-assisted. Grease six-hole (¾-cup/ 180ml) muffin tray or spray six large disposable muffin cases and place on an oven tray.
2   Sift flour into large bowl; add sugar then combined extract, egg, butter, milk and rind. Add berries; stir through gently.
3   Divide muffin mixture among holes of prepared tray.
4   Bake muffins about 35 minutes. Stand muffins in tray for a few minutes before turning onto wire rack.

prep and cook time 45 minutes
makes 6

Chocolate brownie muffins

2 cups (300g) self-raising flour
⅓ cup (35g) cocoa powder
⅓ cup (75g) caster sugar
60g butter, melted
½ cup (95g) chocolate chips
½ cup (75g) chopped pistachios
½ cup (125ml) Nutella
1 egg, lightly beaten
¾ cup (180ml) milk
½ cup (125ml) soured cream

1   Preheat oven to 200°C/180°C fan-assisted. Grease 12-hole (⅓-cup/ 80ml) muffin tray.
2   Sift dry ingredients into large bowl, stir in remaining ingredients.
3   Spoon mixture into prepared tray. Bake muffins about 20 minutes.

prep and cook time 1 hour 35 minutes
makes 12

YOU WILL NEED ABOUT TWO
SMALL OVERRIPE BANANAS
FOR THIS RECIPE

Banana maple muffins

2 cups (300g) self-raising flour
⅓ cup (50g) plain flour
½ teaspoon bicarbonate of soda
½ cup (110g) firmly packed brown sugar
¼ cup (60ml) maple-flavoured syrup
⅔ cup mashed banana
2 eggs, beaten lightly
1 cup (250ml) buttermilk
⅓ cup (80ml) vegetable oil
coconut topping
15g butter
1 tablespoon maple-flavoured syrup
⅔ cup (30g) flaked coconut

1 Preheat oven to 200°C/180°C fan-assisted. Grease 12-hole (⅓-cup/
80ml) muffin tray. Make coconut topping.
2 Sift dry ingredients into large bowl. Stir in maple syrup and banana,
then egg, buttermilk and oil. Do not over-mix; mixture should be
lumpy. Spoon mixture into tray; sprinkle with coconut topping.
3 Bake muffins about 20 minutes.
coconut topping Melt butter in small pan, add syrup and coconut;
stir constantly over high heat until coconut is browned lightly.

prep and cook time 40 minutes
makes 12

White chocolate & macadamia muffins

2 cups (300g) self-raising flour
⅔ cup (150g) caster sugar
¾ cup (140g) white chocolate chips
½ cup (75g) chopped macadamias, toasted
60g butter, melted
¾ cup (180ml) milk
1 egg, lightly beaten

1 Preheat oven to 200°C/180°C fan-assisted. Grease six-hole (¾-cup/
180ml) muffin tray.
2 Sift dry ingredients into large bowl, stir in remaining ingredients.
3 Spoon mixture into prepared tray. Bake muffins about 25 minutes.

prep and cook time 40 minutes
makes 6

Crusty cheese & onion muffins

¼ cup (35g) plain flour
20g butter
1 teaspoon water, approximately
1 tablespoon vegetable oil
1 medium (150g) onion, halved, sliced
1¾ cups (260g) self-raising flour
¾ cup (110g) plain flour, extra
¾ cup (90g) grated cheddar cheese
1 tablespoon chopped fresh chives
1 egg, lightly beaten
1¼ cups (310ml) buttermilk
½ cup (125ml) vegetable oil, extra
chive butter
40g cream cheese, softened
50g butter, softened
2 teaspoons lemon juice
1 tablespoon chopped fresh chives

1   Place plain flour in small bowl, rub in butter, mix in just enough water to bind ingredients. Press dough into a ball, cover, freeze about 30 minutes or until firm.
2   Preheat oven to 200°C/180°C fan-assisted. Grease six-hole (¾-cup/180ml) muffin tray.
3   Heat oil in frying pan, add onion, cook, stirring, until soft and lightly browned; cool.
4   Sift self-raising and extra plain flour into large bowl, stir in half the onion, half the cheese and all the chives, then egg, buttermilk and extra oil.
5   Spoon mixture into prepared tray. Grate frozen dough into small bowl, quickly mix in remaining onion and cheese; sprinkle over muffins. Bake muffins about 25 minutes. Serve with chive butter.
chive butter   Beat cheese and butter together in a small bowl until smooth, stir in juice and chives.

prep and cook time 40 minutes
makes 6

Prosciutto, basil & tomato muffins

5 slices (75g) prosciutto
2½ cups (375g) self-raising flour
90g butter
1 egg, lightly beaten
1¼ cups (310ml) buttermilk
⅓ cup (80ml) milk
⅓ cup (50g) drained chopped sun-dried tomatoes
2 tablespoons chopped fresh basil leaves
1 clove garlic, crushed
1 teaspoon cracked black pepper
1 tablespoon olive oil

1 Preheat oven to 200°C/180°C fan-assisted. Grease six-hole (¾-cup/180ml) muffin tray. Cut prosciutto into strips.
2 Sift flour into large bowl, rub in butter, stir in egg, buttermilk, milk, tomatoes, basil, garlic and pepper.
3 Spoon mixture into prepared tray, top with prosciutto, brush lightly with oil. Bake muffins about 20 minutes. Cover with foil, bake a further 10 minutes.

prep and cook time 45 minutes
makes 6

Arrabbiata muffins

3 (120g) bacon rashers, finely chopped
2 cups (300g) self-raising flour
1 cup (150g) plain flour
⅓ cup (25g) coarsely grated fresh parmesan cheese
¾ cup (90g) pitted sliced black olives
2 tablespoons shredded fresh basil leaves
1 tablespoon chopped fresh oregano
2 eggs, lightly beaten
2 tablespoons tomato purée
3 teaspoons sambal oelek
3 cloves garlic, crushed
¾ cup (180ml) vegetable oil
1½ cups (375ml) buttermilk
1 tablespoon shredded fresh basil leaves, extra

1   Preheat oven to 200°C/180°C fan-assisted. Grease 12-hole (⅓-cup/ 80ml) muffin tray. Cook bacon in heated pan until crisp, drain on absorbent paper, allow to cool.
2   Sift flours into large bowl, stir in bacon, cheese, olives and herbs, then eggs, purée, sambal oelek, garlic, oil and buttermilk.
3   Spoon mixture into prepared tray, sprinkle with extra basil. Bake muffins about 20 minutes.

prep and cook time 40 minutes
makes 12

Ham & cheese muffins

2 cups (300g) self-raising flour
½ teaspoon chicken stock powder
½ teaspoon ground hot paprika
80g butter
6 slices (130g) ham, chopped
1½ cups (185g) coarsely grated cheddar cheese
1 egg, lightly beaten
1 cup (250ml) milk
ground hot paprika, extra

1   Preheat oven to 200°C/180°C fan-assisted. Grease 12-hole (⅓-cup/ 80ml) muffin tray.
2   Sift dry ingredients into large bowl, rub in butter. Stir in ham and cheese, then egg and milk.
3   Spoon mixture into prepared tray, sprinkle with a little extra paprika. Bake muffins about 20 minutes.

prep and cook time 35 minutes
makes 12

Arrabbiata Muffins

Scones

Fruity scones

PULL-APART SCONES
with caramel sauce

BUTTERMILK SCONES

savoury CHEESE SCONES

LIGHT, FLUFFY SCONES SERVED
HOT FROM THE OVEN WITH
BUTTER OR JAM AND CREAM
ARE A DELIGHT FOR MORNING
OR AFTERNOON TEA

Sultana scones

2½ cups (375g) self-raising flour
1 tablespoon caster sugar
30g butter
½ cup (80g) sultanas
2 teaspoons finely grated lemon rind
¾ cup (180ml) milk
½ cup (125ml) water, approximately

1   Preheat oven to 220°C/200°C fan-assisted. Grease deep 19cm-square cake tin.
2   Sift flour and sugar into large bowl; rub in butter with fingertips. Stir in sultanas and rind.
3   Make a well in centre of flour mixture; add milk and almost all the water. Using a knife, 'cut' the milk and water through the flour mixture to mix to a soft, sticky dough. Knead dough on floured surface until smooth.
4   Press dough out to a 2cm thickness. Dip 4.5cm cutter into flour; cut as many rounds as you can from the piece of dough. Place scones side by side, just touching, in tin. Gently knead scraps of dough together; repeat pressing and cutting of dough. Place in same tin. Brush tops with a little extra milk.
5   Bake scones about 15 minutes or until just browned and scones sound hollow when tapped firmly on the top with fingers.

prep and cook time 55 minutes
makes 16

Buttermilk scones

2½ cups (375g) self-raising flour
1 tablespoon caster sugar
30g butter
1¼ cups (310ml) buttermilk, approximately

1   Preheat oven to 220°C/200°C fan-assisted. Grease deep 19cm-square cake tin.
2   Sift flour and sugar into large bowl; rub in butter with fingertips.
3   Make well in centre of flour mixture; add buttermilk. Using a knife, 'cut' the buttermilk through the flour mixture to mix to a soft, sticky dough. Knead dough on floured surface until smooth.
4   Press dough out to a 2cm thickness. Dip 4.5cm cutter into flour; cut as many rounds as you can from the piece of dough. Place scones side by side, just touching, in tin. Gently knead scraps of dough together; repeat pressing and cutting of dough. Place in same tin. Brush tops with a little extra milk.
5   Bake scones about 15 minutes or until just browned and scones sound hollow when tapped firmly on the top with fingers.

prep and cook time 35 minutes
makes 16

Honey & muesli scones

2½ cups (375g) self-raising flour
1 teaspoon ground cinnamon
1 tablespoon caster sugar
30g butter
½ cup (65g) toasted muesli
¼ cup (90g) honey
¾ cup (180ml) milk

1 Preheat oven to 220°C/200°C fan-assisted. Grease deep 19cm-square cake tin.
2 Sift flour, cinnamon and sugar into large bowl; rub in butter with fingertips. Add muesli.
3 Make a well in centre of flour mixture; add honey and milk. Using a knife, 'cut' the milk through the flour mixture to mix to a soft, sticky dough. Knead dough on floured surface until smooth.
4 Press dough out to 2cm thickness. Dip 4.5cm cutter into flour; cut as many rounds as you can from the piece of dough. Place scones side by side, just touching, in tin. Gently knead scraps of dough together; repeat pressing and cutting of dough. Place in same tin. Brush tops with a little extra milk.
5 Bake scones about 15 minutes or until browned and scones sound hollow when tapped firmly on the top with fingers.

prep and cook time 40 minutes
makes 16

THE FEAR-OF-FAILURE-FACTOR
SURROUNDING SCONES IS VERY
HIGH. BUT ONCE YOU'VE GOT THE
HANG OF THEM, YOU'LL FIND
THEM INCREDIBLY EASY
TO MAKE.

Cardamom marmalade scones

2½ cups (375g) self-raising flour
1 tablespoon caster sugar
30g butter
1 teaspoon ground cardamom
2 teaspoons finely grated orange rind
1 cup (250ml) milk
⅓ cup (115g) orange marmalade

1 Preheat oven to 220°C/200°C fan-assisted. Grease deep 19cm-square cake tin.
2 Sift flour and sugar into large bowl; rub in butter with fingertips. Stir in cardamom and rind.
3 Make a well in centre of flour mixture; add combined milk and marmalade. Using a knife, 'cut' the milk and marmalade through the flour mixture to mix to a soft, sticky dough. Knead dough on floured surface until smooth.
4 Press dough out to a 2cm thickness. Dip 4.5cm cutter into flour; cut as many rounds as you can from the piece of dough. Place scones side by side, just touching, in tin. Gently knead scraps of dough together; repeat pressing and cutting of dough. Place in same tin. Brush tops with a little extra milk.
5 Bake scones about 15 minutes or until browned and scones sound hollow when tapped firmly on the top with fingers.

prep and cook time 40 minutes
makes 16

IF YOU'RE TROUBLED BY TINY WHITE SPECKS ON TOP OF YOUR SCONES – IT'S ONLY UNDISSOLVED SUGAR GRAINS, USE ICING SUGAR INSTEAD OF CASTER SUGAR.

Cranberry, oatmeal & cinnamon scones

1 cup (160g) wholemeal self-raising flour
1 cup (150g) white self-raising flour
1 teaspoon ground cinnamon
½ cup (70g) fine oatmeal
½ teaspoon finely grated lemon rind
30g butter
¾ cup (105g) dried cranberries
1 cup (250ml) milk
2 tablespoons honey
1 tablespoon oatmeal, extra

1 Preheat oven to 220°C/200°C fan-assisted. Grease and flour deep 19cm-square cake tin.

2 Sift flours and cinnamon into a medium bowl, add oatmeal and rind; rub in butter with fingertips. Stir in cranberries.

3 Make a well in centre of flour mixture; add combined milk and honey. Using a knife, 'cut' the milk and honey through the flour mixture to mix to a soft, sticky dough. Knead dough on floured surface until smooth.

4 Press dough out to 2cm thickness. Dip 5.5cm cutter into flour; cut as many rounds as you can from the piece of dough. Place scones side by side, just touching, in tin. Gently knead scraps of dough together; repeat pressing and cutting of dough. Place in same tin. Brush tops with a little extra milk; sprinkle with extra oatmeal.

5 Bake scones about 15 minutes or until browned and scones sound hollow when tapped firmly on the top with fingers.

prep and cook time 35 minutes
makes 12

THE PURPOSE OF GLAZING SCONES IS TO BRUSH AWAY ANY EXCESS FLOUR, AND TO DRAW THE HEAT FROM THE OVEN TO THE SCONES TO BROWN THE TOPS. EGG YOLK WILL GIVE THE DARKEST COLOUR, WATER THE PALEST COLOUR, MILK WILL GIVE A GOOD MIDDLE OF THE ROAD COLOUR.

Blueberry ginger scones

2½ cups (375g) self-raising flour
1 tablespoon caster sugar
30g butter
3 teaspoons ground ginger
½ cup (75g) fresh or frozen blueberries
¾ cup (180ml) milk
½ cup (125ml) water, approximately

1 Preheat oven to 220°C/200°C fan-assisted. Grease deep 19cm-square cake tin.
2 Sift flour and sugar into large bowl; rub in butter with fingertips. Stir in ginger and blueberries.
3 Make a well in centre of flour mixture; add combined milk and almost all of the water. Using a knife, 'cut' the milk and water through the flour mixture to mix to a soft, sticky dough. Knead dough on floured surface until smooth.
4 Press dough out to a 2cm thickness. Dip 4.5cm cutter into flour; cut as many rounds as you can from the piece of dough. Place scones side by side, just touching, in tin. Gently knead scraps of dough together; repeat pressing and cutting of dough. Place in same tin. Brush tops with a little extra milk.
5 Bake scones about 15 minutes or until browned and scones sound hollow when tapped firmly on the top with fingers.

prep and cook time 40 minutes
makes 16

WE LIKE TO BAKE SCONES IN A TIN WITH SIDES. THE SCONES WILL TAKE A LITTLE LONGER TO BAKE IN THESE TINS THAN THOSE BAKED ON A FLAT BAKING TRAY. GREASE THE TINS EVENLY.

Apricot & almond scones

2½ cups (375g) self-raising flour
1 tablespoon caster sugar
30g butter
1 teaspoon mixed spice
1 cup (150g) finely chopped dried apricots
⅓ cup (45g) finely chopped roasted slivered almonds
¾ cup (180ml) milk
½ cup (125ml) water, approximately

1 Preheat oven to 220°C/200°C fan-assisted. Grease deep 19cm-square cake tin.

2 Sift flour and sugar into large bowl; rub in butter with fingertips. Stir in spice, apricots and nuts.

3 Make a well in centre of flour mixture; add combined milk and almost all of the water. Using a knife, 'cut' the milk and water through the flour mixture to mix to a soft, sticky dough. Knead dough on floured surface until smooth.

4 Press dough out to a 2cm thickness. Dip 4.5cm cutter into flour; cut as many rounds as you can from the piece of dough. Place scones side by side, just touching, in tin. Gently knead scraps of dough together; repeat pressing and cutting of dough. Place in same tin. Brush tops with a little extra milk.

5 Bake scones about 15 minutes or until just browned and scones sound hollow when tapped firmly on the top with fingers.

prep and cook time 40 minutes
makes 16

Cheese scones

1½ cups (225g) self-raising flour
¼ teaspoon cayenne pepper
2 teaspoons caster sugar
⅓ cup (25g) finely grated parmesan cheese
1 cup (120g) coarsely grated cheddar cheese
1 cup (250ml) milk, approximately
40g butter, melted
herb butter
60g butter, softened
1 tablespoon finely chopped fresh mixed herbs

1　Preheat oven to 220°C/200°C fan-assisted. Grease 20cm-round sandwich cake tin.
2　Sift flour, pepper and sugar into medium bowl, add parmesan and half of the cheddar; stir in enough milk to make a soft, sticky dough. Knead dough on floured surface until smooth.
3　Press dough out to 2cm thickness. Dip 3.5cm round cutter in flour; cut as many rounds as you can from dough. Place scones, side by side, just touching, in tin. Gently knead scraps of dough together; repeat pressing and cutting of dough, place in same tin. Brush tops with melted butter; sprinkle with remaining cheddar.
4　Bake scones about 20 minutes or until browned and scones sound hollow when tapped firmly on the top with fingers.
5　Meanwhile, make herb butter.
6　Serve warm scones with herb butter.
herb butter　Combine ingredients in small bowl.

prep and cook time 30 minutes
makes 24

SCONES ARE DONE WHEN THEY SOUND HOLLOW, WHEN THEY'RE TAPPED FIRMLY ON THE TOP. TEST THE SCONES IN THE MIDDLE OF THE TIN, AS THESE TAKE THE LONGEST TO COOK. AS SOON AS THEY'RE OUT OF THE OVEN, SHAKE THE TIN TO FREE THEM FROM THE BASE AND SIDES; TURN ONTO A TEA TOWEL, COVER WITH ANOTHER TEA TOWEL TO SOFTEN SCONES. FOR CRISP-SIDED SCONES, TURN THEM ONTO A WIRE RACK TO COOL.

Spicy fruit tea scones

1¼ cups (310ml) hot strong strained black tea
¾ cup (135g) mixed dried fruit
3 cups (450g) self-raising flour
1 teaspoon ground cinnamon
1 teaspoon mixed spice
2 tablespoons caster sugar
20g butter
½ cup (120g) soured cream, approximately

1   Preheat oven to 220°C/200°C fan-assisted. Grease 23cm-square cake tin.

2   Combine tea and fruit in small heatproof bowl, cover, let stand 20 minutes or until mixture is cooled to room temperature.

3   Sift dry ingredients into large bowl; rub in butter with fingertips. Stir in fruit mixture and enough soured cream to mix to a soft, sticky dough. Knead dough on floured surface until smooth.

4   Press dough out evenly to 2cm thickness. Dip 5.5cm cutter into flour; cut as many rounds as you can from piece of dough. Place scones side by side, just touching, in tin. Gently knead scraps of dough together; repeat pressing and cutting out of dough, place in same tin. Brush tops with a little milk.

5   Bake scones about 15 minutes or until browned and scones sound hollow when tapped firmly on the top with fingers.

prep and cook time 35 minutes
(plus standing time)
makes 16

YOU'RE AIMING FOR A SOFT, STICKY DOUGH THAT JUST HOLDS ITS SHAPE WHEN TURNED OUT OF THE BOWL. AVOID OVERHANDLING AND USING TOO MUCH FLOUR WHICH CAN UPSET THE BALANCE OF INGREDIENTS.

Caramel apple pull-apart

2 cups (300g) self-raising flour
30g butter
1 cup (250ml) milk, approximately
⅓ cup (65g) firmly packed brown sugar
400g can pie apples
pinch ground nutmeg
½ teaspoon ground cinnamon
2 tablespoons coarsely chopped toasted pecans
caramel sauce
¼ cup (60ml) double cream
20g butter
½ cup (100g) firmly packed brown sugar

1 Preheat oven to 200°C/180°C fan-assisted. Grease deep 22cm-round cake tin.

2 Sift flour into medium bowl; rub in butter with fingertips.

3 Make a well in centre of flour mixture; add enough milk to mix to a soft, sticky dough. Knead dough on floured surface until smooth.

4 Roll dough on floured baking paper to 21cm x 40cm rectangle. Sprinkle dough with sugar, spread with combined apples and spices to within 3cm from long edge. Using paper as a guide, roll dough up like a swiss roll, from long side. Use a floured, serrated knife to cut roll into 12 slices. Place 11 slices upright around edge of tin; place remaining slice in centre.

5 Bake pull-apart about 25 minutes. Stand a few minutes before turning onto wire rack.

6 Meanwhile, make caramel sauce.

7 Brush hot pull-apart evenly with caramel sauce, sprinkle with nuts.

caramel sauce Stir ingredients in small saucepan constantly over heat, without boiling, until sugar is dissolved. Simmer, uncovered, without stirring, about 3 minutes or until mixture is thickened slightly.

prep and cook time 1 hour
makes 12

Pastries

ROASTED PEAR TART
golden & buttery

Nutty pecan pies

TANGY LEMON TART

old-fashioned
APPLE PIE

FROM HOMELY BLACKBERRY AND
APPLE PIE TO ELEGANT RHUBARB
GALETTES, THERE'S SOMETHING
HERE FOR EVERYONE – SO WHO
DID EAT ALL THE PIES?

Old-fashioned apple pie

1 cup (150g) plain flour
½ cup (75g) self-raising flour
¼ cup (35g) cornflour
¼ cup (30g) custard powder
2 tablespoons caster sugar
125g chilled butter, chopped
1 egg, separated
¼ cup (60ml) iced water, approximately
lemony apple filling
7 large apples (1.5kg)
½ cup (125ml) water
2 tablespoons sugar
¼ teaspoon ground cinnamon
1 teaspoon grated lemon rind

1   Make lemony apple filling.
2   Blend or process flours, custard powder, half the sugar and all the butter until combined. Add egg yolk and enough of the water to make ingredients just come together. Knead dough on lightly floured surface until smooth. Wrap in cling film; refrigerate 30 minutes.
3   Roll two-thirds of the dough between sheets of baking parchment until large enough to line 23cm-round pie dish. Ease dough into dish; trim edge. Cover; refrigerate 30 minutes.
4   Preheat oven to 180°C/160°C fan-assisted.
5   Roll remaining pastry between sheets of baking parchment until large enough to cover pie; discard pastry scraps.
6   Spoon lemony apple filling evenly into pastry case; brush edge of pastry with some of the lightly beaten egg white. Cover filling with pastry sheet. Press edges together firmly; trim using knife. Using fingers, pinch edges to make a frill. Brush pastry with a little remaining egg white. Sprinkle pie evenly with remaining sugar.
7   Bake for 40 minutes or until pie is golden brown.
lemony apple filling   Peel apples; cut into quarters. Remove cores; cut each quarter in half lengthways. Place apples in large saucepan with the water; bring to a boil. Reduce heat; cover. Cook about 5 minutes or until apples are just tender. Transfer apples to large bowl; gently stir in sugar, cinnamon and lemon rind. Cool to room temperature.

prep and cook time 1 hour 40 minutes
(plus refrigeration and cooling time)
serves 8

Blackberry & apple pie

9 medium apples (1.5kg)
2 tablespoons caster sugar
1 tablespoon cornflour
1 tablespoon water
300g frozen blackberries
1 tablespoon cornflour, extra
1 tablespoon demerara sugar
pastry
2 cups (300g) plain flour
⅔ cup (110g) icing sugar
185g chilled butter, chopped
2 egg yolks
1 tablespoon iced water,
approximately

1 Peel and core apples; slice thinly. Place in large saucepan with caster sugar; cook, covered, over low heat, about 10 minutes or until apples are just tender. Strain over small saucepan; reserve cooking liquid.

2 Blend cornflour with the water, stir into reserved cooking liquid over heat until mixture boils and thickens. Place apples in large bowl, gently stir in cornflour mixture; cool to room temperature.

3 Meanwhile, make pastry.

4 Preheat oven to 220°C/210°C fan-assisted.

5 Toss blackberries in extra cornflour; stir gently into apple mixture.

6 Spoon fruit mixture into pastry case; top with rolled pastry. Press edges together, trim with knife; decorate edge. Brush pastry with a little water; sprinkle with demerara sugar. Using knife, make three cuts in top of pastry to allow steam to escape.

7 Place pie on oven tray; bake, uncovered, for 20 minutes. Reduce oven temperature to 200°C/180°C fan-assisted; bake, uncovered, for about 30 minutes or until pastry is browned lightly. Cool 10 minutes before serving.

pastry Blend or process flour, icing sugar and butter until combined. Add egg yolks and enough of the water to make ingredients just come together. Knead dough on lightly floured surface until smooth. Wrap in cling film, refrigerate 30 minutes. Roll two-thirds of the dough between sheets of baking parchment until large enough to line 23cm-round pie dish. Ease dough into dish; trim edge. Cover; refrigerate 30 minutes. Roll remaining pastry between sheets of baking parchment until large enough to cover pie.

prep and cook time 2 hours
(plus refrigeration and cooling time)
serves 8

WE USED GOLDEN DELICIOUS
APPLES IN THIS RECIPE.
FOR A DIFFERENT FLAVOUR,
REPLACE BLACKBERRIES WITH
BLUEBERRIES, RASPBERRIES
OR STRAWBERRIES.

Apple cream pie

2 medium green apples (300g), peeled, sliced thinly
2 eggs
½ cup (110g) caster sugar
2 tablespoons plain flour
2 teaspoons grated lemon rind
1¾ cups (425ml) double cream
250g cream cheese, softened
1 tablespoon mixed peel
¼ cup (40g) raisins, chopped finely
1 teaspoon ground cinnamon
pastry
1¼ cups (185g) plain flour
½ teaspoon ground cinnamon
¼ cup (55g) caster sugar
1 teaspoon baking powder
2 teaspoons grated lemon rind
125g chilled butter, chopped coarsely
1 egg yolk
2 tablespoons dry sherry

1   Preheat oven to 180°C/160°C fan-assisted.
Make pastry.
2   Arrange apple in overlapping lines in pastry case.
Beat eggs and sugar in small bowl with electric mixer
until thick; gradually add flour, beating well between
additions. Add rind, ½ cup (125ml) of the cream,
cream cheese, peel and raisins; mix well.
3   Pour filling over apples; bake pie 45 minutes;
allow to cool.
4   Beat remaining cream; spread evenly over top
of pie. Sprinkle with cinnamon.
pastry Combine flour, cinnamon, sugar, baking
powder and rind in medium bowl; rub in
butter. Beat egg yolk and sherry in small bowl
until combined. Add to flour mixture; mix well.
Spread dough evenly over base of 19cm x 29cm
rectangular cake tin.

prep and cook time 1 hour 30 minutes
(plus cooling time)
serves 10

Roast nectarine tart

8 nectarines (1.5kg), halved, stone removed
¼ cup (60ml) orange juice
½ cup (110g) firmly packed brown sugar
pastry
1⅔ cups (250g) plain flour
⅔ cup (110g) icing sugar
125g chilled butter, chopped
1 egg yolk
1½ tablespoons cold water, approximately
crème patissiere
300ml whipping cream
1 cup (250ml) milk
½ cup (110g) caster sugar
1 vanilla pod
3 egg yolks
2 tablespoons cornflour
90g unsalted butter, chopped

1 Grease 19cm x 27cm loose-based flan tin. Make pastry.
2 Make crème pâtissière while pastry case is cooling.
3 Increase oven temperature to 220°C/200°C fan-assisted. Place nectarines, in single layer, in large shallow baking dish; sprinkle with juice and sugar. Roast, uncovered, about 20 minutes or until nectarines are soft. Cool.
4 Meanwhile, spoon crème pâtissière into pastry case, cover; refrigerate about 30 minutes or until firm. Top with nectarines.
pastry Blend or process flour, sugar and butter until combined. Add egg yolk and enough of the water to make ingredients just come together. Knead dough on floured surface until smooth. Cover; refrigerate 30 minutes. Preheat oven to 180°C/160°C fan-assisted. Roll dough between sheets of baking parchment until large enough to line prepared tin. Ease dough into prepared tin, press into sides; trim edges. Cover; refrigerate 30 minutes. Cover pastry case with baking parchment, fill with dried beans or rice; place on oven tray. Bake, uncovered, 10 minutes. Remove paper and beans; bake, uncovered, about 10 minutes or until pastry case is browned lightly. Cool.

crème patissiere Combine cream, milk and sugar in medium saucepan. Split vanilla pod in half lengthways, scrape seeds into saucepan, then add pod; bring to a boil. Remove from heat; discard pod. Beat egg yolks in small bowl with electric mixer until thick and creamy; beat in cornflour. Gradually beat in hot cream mixture. Strain mixture into same cleaned saucepan; stir over heat until mixture boils and thickens. Remove from heat; whisk in butter. Cover surface of custard with cling film; cool to room temperature.

prep and cook time 1 hour 25 minutes (plus refrigeration time)
serves 8

Pecan, macadamia & walnut pies

1¼ cups (185g) plain flour
⅓ cup (55g) icing sugar
¼ cup (30g) ground almonds
125g chilled butter, chopped
1 egg yolk
filling
⅓ cup (50g) macadamias, toasted
⅓ cup (45g) pecans, toasted
⅓ cup (35g) walnuts, toasted
2 tablespoons brown sugar
1 tablespoon plain flour
40g butter, melted
2 eggs, beaten lightly
¾ cup (180ml) maple syrup

1 Grease four 10cm-round loose-based flan tins.
2 Blend or process flour, icing sugar, ground almonds and butter until combined. Add egg yolk; process until ingredients just come together. Knead dough on lightly floured surface until smooth. Wrap in cling film, refrigerate 30 minutes.
3 Divide pastry into quarters. Roll each piece, between sheets of baking parchment, into rounds large enough to line prepared tins; lift pastry into each tin. Press into sides; trim edges. Cover; refrigerate 30 minutes.
4 Meanwhile, preheat oven to 200°C/180°C fan-assisted.
5 Place tins on oven tray. Line each tin with baking parchment, fill with dried beans or rice. Bake, uncovered, for 10 minutes. Remove paper and beans. Bake, uncovered, further 7 minutes or until pastry cases are browned lightly.
6 Reduce oven temperature to 180°C/160°C fan-assisted.
7 Divide filling among cases. Bake for 25 minutes or until set; cool.
filling Combine ingredients in medium bowl; mix well.

prep and cook time 1 hour 5 minutes
(plus refrigeration time)
serves 4

TO TOAST NUTS, PLACE IN A HEAVY-BASED FRYING PAN, STIR CONSTANTLY OVER MEDIUM-TO-HIGH HEAT, UNTIL NUTS ARE EVENLY BROWNED. REMOVE FROM PAN IMMEDIATELY.

Roasted pear tart

3 medium pears (700g)
1 tablespoon maple syrup
¼ cup (55g) raw sugar
40g butter, chopped
1 sheet ready rolled butter-puff pastry
1 egg, beaten lightly

1   Preheat oven to 180°C/160°C fan-assisted.
2   Peel pears, leaving stems intact; cut in half lengthways. Remove cores carefully. Place pears in baking dish, cut-side up; top with syrup, sugar and butter.
3   Bake pears about 20 minutes or until tender, brushing pears occasionally with pan juices and turning the pears over after 10 minutes.
4   Increase oven temperature to 200°C/180°C fan-assisted.
5   Cut pastry sheet in half; place pastry halves about 2cm apart on greased oven tray.
6   Place 3 pear halves, cut-side down, on each pastry half. Brush pears and pastry with pan juices, then brush pastry only with a little of the egg.
7   Bake for about 20 minutes or until pastry is puffed and browned lightly. To serve, cut pastry so each serving contains a pear half.

prep and cook time 1 hour
serves 6

GOLDEN, GLAZED PEARS ON A SIMPLE PASTRY BASE. SERVE WITH ICE-CREAM OR HOT CUSTARD.

Mince tarts

2 cups (300g) plain flour
2 tablespoons custard powder
⅓ cup (75g) caster sugar
185g chilled butter, chopped
1 egg yolk
2 tablespoons cold water, approximately
1 egg white, beaten lightly
1 tablespoon sugar
mincemeat filling
475g jar mincemeat
2 tablespoons brandy
¼ cup (35g) glacé peaches, chopped
¼ cup (35g) glacé apricots, chopped
1 teaspoon grated orange rind
2 teaspoons grated lemon rind

1   Grease two 12-hole deep bun trays.
2   Blend or process flour, custard powder, sugar and butter until combined. Add egg yolk and enough of the water to make ingredients just come together. Knead dough on lightly floured surface until smooth. Cover in cling film; refrigerate 30 minutes.
3   Roll two-thirds of the dough between sheets of baking parchment until 3mm thick. Cut 24 x 7.5cm rounds from pastry, re-roll pastry if necessary to make 24 rounds. Place rounds into greased trays, reserve the pastry scraps. Cover, refrigerate while preparing the filling.
4   Prepare mincemeat filling.
5   Preheat oven to 200°C/180°C fan-assisted.
6   Spoon 1 heaped teaspoon of mincemeat filling into pastry cases. Roll remaining pastry until 3mm thick. Using 4.5cm star and Christmas tree cutters, cut out 12 stars and 12 trees. Place pastry shapes in centre of tarts; brush with egg white, sprinkle with sugar.
7   Bake about 20 minutes or until browned lightly.
mincemeat filling Combine ingredients in medium bowl.

prep and cook time 1 hour 20 minutes
makes 24

TRADITIONAL AT CHRISTMAS, BUT
DELICIOUS ALL YEAR ROUND, SERVE
MINCE PIES HOT WITH A DOLLOP OF
LIQUEUR CREAM OR BRANDY BUTTER

Lemon tart

1¼ cups (185g) plain flour
¼ cup (40g) icing sugar
¼ cup (30g) ground almonds
125g chilled butter, chopped
1 egg yolk
lemon filling
1 tablespoon finely grated lemon rind
½ cup (125ml) lemon juice
5 eggs
¾ cup (165g) caster sugar
1 cup (250ml) whipping cream

1 Blend or process flour, icing sugar, ground almonds and butter until combined. Add egg yolk, process until ingredients just come together. Knead dough on lightly floured surface until smooth. Wrap in cling film, refrigerate 30 minutes.

2 Roll pastry between sheets of baking parchment until large enough to line 24cm-round loose-based flan tin. Ease dough into tin; trim edge. Cover; refrigerate 30 minutes.

3 Meanwhile, preheat oven to 200°C/180°C fan-assisted.

4 Place tin on oven tray. Line pastry case with baking parchment, fill with dried beans or rice. Bake, uncovered, for 15 minutes. Remove paper and beans; bake, uncovered, further 10 minutes or until browned lightly.

5 Meanwhile, make lemon filling.

6 Reduce oven to 180°C/160°C fan-assisted.

7 Pour lemon filling into pastry case, bake for about 30 minutes or until filling has set slightly; cool.

8 Refrigerate until cold. Serve dusted with sifted icing sugar.

lemon filling Whisk ingredients in medium bowl; stand 5 minutes.

prep and cook time 1 hour 25 minutes
(plus refrigeration and cooling time)
serves 8

YOU WILL NEED ABOUT THREE MEDIUM LEMONS FOR THIS TART. WHEN LINING THE FLAN TIN, USE A KNIFE TO CLEANLY TRIM THE EDGES OF THE PASTRY SHELL.

Peach & macadamia tart

1¼ cups (185g) plain flour
2 tablespoons caster sugar
90g chilled butter, chopped
1 egg yolk
½ teaspoon vanilla extract
2 teaspoons cold water, approximately
3 medium peaches (500g), cut into eighths
macadamia filling
¾ cup (110g) macadamias
¼ cup (35g) plain flour
75g butter
⅓ cup (75g) firmly packed brown sugar
1 egg
1 egg yolk
2 tablespoons maple syrup

1   Blend or process flour, sugar and butter until combined. Add egg yolk, extract and enough of the water to make ingredients just come together. Knead dough on lightly floured surface until smooth. Wrap in cling film; refrigerate 30 minutes.
2   Roll dough between sheets of baking parchment until large enough to line the base and side of 24cm-round, loose-based flan tin. Ease dough into tin; trim edge. Place flan tin on oven tray; cover, refrigerate 30 minutes.
3   Meanwhile, preheat oven to 180°C/160°C fan-assisted.
4   Line pastry case with baking parchment, fill with dried beans or rice. Bake, uncovered, for 20 minutes. Remove paper and beans; bake, uncovered, further 5 minutes or until browned lightly.
5   Meanwhile, make macadamia filling.
6   Spread macadamia filling into pastry case; arrange peach segments over filling. Bake about 35 minutes or until golden brown and firm to touch. Cool.
macadamia filling Process macadamias and 2 tablespoons of the flour until fine. Beat butter and sugar in small bowl with electric mixer until pale. Beat in egg and egg yolk until combined, then fold in syrup, macadamia mixture and remaining flour.

prep and cook time 1 hour 30 minutes
(plus refrigeration and cooling time)
serves 8

THESE TRADITIONAL PARISIAN
SPECIALTIES ARE NAMED AFTER A
PALM TREE BECAUSE, WHEN BAKED,
THEY RESEMBLE PALM FRONDS.
QUICK AND EASY, THEY'RE GREAT
FOR AFTERNOON TEA.

Palmiers

2 tablespoons caster sugar, approximately
2 sheets ready-rolled puff pastry, thawed

1 Sprinkle worktop with a little sugar. Using rolling pin press pastry gently into sugar. Fold two opposing sides of pastry inwards to meet in the middle. Sprinkle with a little more sugar, fold in half again so edges just touch in the middle; flatten slightly. Repeat process with remaining pastry and sugar; cover, refrigerate 30 minutes.
2 Meanwhile, preheat oven to 200°C/180°C fan-assisted.
3 Cut pastry roll into 1.5cm slices; place slices about 10cm apart on lightly greased oven trays.
4 Bake for 10 minutes. Turn palmiers with fish slice; bake further 10 minutes or until crisp. Lift onto wire racks to cool.

prep and cook time 35 minutes (plus refrigeration time)
makes 32

Rhubarb galette

You need about four trimmed large stems of rhubarb (250g) for this recipe.

20g butter, melted
2½ cups (275g) coarsely chopped rhubarb
⅓ cup (75g) firmly packed brown sugar
1 teaspoon finely grated orange rind
1 sheet ready-rolled puff pastry
2 tablespoons ground almonds
10g butter, melted, extra

1 Preheat oven to 220°C/210°C fan-assisted. Line oven tray with baking parchment.
2 Combine butter, rhubarb, sugar and rind in medium bowl.
3 Cut 24cm round from pastry, place on prepared tray; sprinkle ground almonds evenly over pastry. Spread rhubarb mixture over pastry, leaving a 4cm border. Fold 2cm of pastry edge up and around filling. Brush edge with extra butter.
4 Bake galette, uncovered, about 20 minutes or until browned lightly.

prep and cook time 30 minutes
serves 4

Biscuits
& Slices

CRISP COOKIES
perfect for dunking

MELT-IN-THE-MOUTH
macaroons

FUDGE BROWNIES

Fruity slices

PERFECT WITH MID-MORNING
COFFEE, AFTERNOON TEA OR
AS AN AFTER-DINNER TREAT,
BISCUITS AND SLICES ARE AN
ALL-ROUND FAVOURITE

Basic vanilla cookies

200g butter, softened
½ teaspoon vanilla extract
1 cup (160g) icing sugar
1 egg
1¾ cups (260g) plain flour
½ teaspoon bicarbonate of soda

1 Preheat oven to 170°C/150°C fan-assisted. Grease oven trays; line with baking parchment.
2 Beat butter, extract, sifted icing sugar and egg in small bowl with electric mixer until light and fluffy. Transfer mixture to medium bowl; stir in sifted flour and soda, in two batches.
3 Roll level tablespoons of dough into balls; place about 3cm apart on oven trays.
4 Bake cookies about 15 minutes; cool on trays.

prep and cook time 35 minutes
makes 30

Variations

cranberry & coconut Stir ½ cup (65g) dried cranberries and ½ cup (40g) shredded coconut into basic cookie mixture before flour and soda are added.
pear & ginger Stir ¼ cup (35g) finely chopped dried pears, ¼ cup (55g) coarsely chopped glacé ginger and ½ cup (45g) rolled oats into basic cookie mixture before flour and soda are added.
spiced choc chip Stir ½ cup (95g) dark chocolate chips into basic cookie mixture before flour and soda are added. Roll level tablespoons of dough into balls then roll balls in a mixture of 1 tablespoon caster sugar, 2 teaspoons ground nutmeg and 2 teaspoons ground cinnamon.
brown sugar & pecan Substitute 1 cup (220g) firmly packed brown sugar for the icing sugar in the basic cookie mixture. Stir ½ cup (60g) coarsely chopped pecans into basic cookie mixture before flour and soda are added.

THESE COOKIES CAN BE FLAVOURED WITH ANY ESSENCE, CITRUS RINDS, FINELY CHOPPED DRIED FRUIT AND NUTS. NOT TO MENTION A WHOLE RANGE OF DIFFERENT FLAVOURED ICINGS TO TOP THEM – THE VARIATIONS ARE ENDLESS.

Left: cranberry & coconut (top); spiced choc chip (middle); pear & ginger (bottom)
Right: brown sugar & pecan

Decadent mocha finger biscuits

1 teaspoon instant coffee granules
2 teaspoons boiling water
125g butter, softened
¾ cup (165g) firmly packed brown sugar
1 egg
1½ cups (225g) plain flour
¼ cup (35g) self-raising flour
¼ cup (25g) cocoa powder
75 roasted coffee beans
mocha custard
2 tablespoons custard powder
2 tablespoons caster sugar
60g dark eating chocolate, chopped roughly
1 cup (250ml) milk
1 tablespoon coffee-flavoured liqueur

1 Blend coffee with the water. Beat butter, sugar and egg in small bowl with electric mixer until combined. Stir in coffee mixture, sifted flours and cocoa, in two batches.
2 Knead dough on floured surface until smooth; roll dough between sheets of baking parchment until 4mm thick. Cover; refrigerate 30 minutes.
3 Preheat oven to 180°C/160°C fan-assisted. Grease oven trays; line with baking parchment.
4 Make mocha custard.
5 Using 8.5cm square cutter, cut out 25 shapes from dough. Halve squares to make 50 rectangles; place on oven trays. Press three coffee beans on half of the rectangles.
6 Bake biscuits about 12 minutes. Cool on wire racks. Spread custard over plain biscuits; top with coffee-bean topped biscuits.

mocha custard Blend custard powder, sugar and chocolate with milk in small saucepan; stir over heat until mixture boils and thickens. Remove from heat, stir in liqueur. Cover surface with cling film; refrigerate until cold.

prep and cook time 50 minutes (plus refrigeration time)
makes 25

Choc-hazelnut cookie sandwiches

80g butter, chopped
1 teaspoon vanilla extract
¼ cup (55g) caster sugar
1 egg
½ cup (50g) ground hazelnuts
¾ cup (110g) plain flour
¼ cup (25g) cocoa powder
1 tablespoon cocoa powder, extra
choc-hazelnut cream
100g dark eating chocolate, melted
50g butter
⅓ cup (110g) Nutella

1 Preheat oven to 180°C/160°C fan-assisted.
2 Beat butter, extract, sugar and egg in small bowl with electric mixer until light and fluffy; stir in ground hazelnuts, sifted flour and cocoa. Wrap dough in cling film; refrigerate about 1 hour or until firm.
3 Roll dough between sheets of baking parchment until 3mm thick. Using 4cm-fluted cutter, cut rounds from dough. Place rounds on lightly greased oven trays.
4 Bake biscuits about 8 minutes. Stand biscuits on trays 5 minutes; transfer to wire rack to cool.
5 Spoon choc-hazelnut cream into piping bag fitted with large fluted tube. Pipe cream onto one biscuit; sandwich with another biscuit. Repeat with remaining biscuits and cream. Dust with extra sifted cocoa powder.
choc-hazelnut cream Beat cooled chocolate, butter and Nutella in small bowl with electric mixer until thick and glossy.

prep and cook time 35 minutes
(plus refrigeration and cooling time)
makes 30

Monte Carlo biscuits

180g butter, softened
1 teaspoon vanilla extract
½ cup (110g) firmly packed brown sugar
1 egg
1¼ cups (185g) self-raising flour
¾ cup (105g) plain flour
¼ teaspoon bicarbonate of soda
⅔ cup (50g) desiccated coconut
⅓ cup (110g) raspberry jam
vienna cream
60g butter
½ teaspoon vanilla extract
¾ cup (120g) icing sugar
2 teaspoons milk

1   Preheat oven to 200°C/180°C fan-assisted. Grease oven trays; line with baking parchment.
2   Beat butter, extract and sugar in small bowl with electric mixer until just combined; beat in egg. Stir in sifted flours, soda and coconut in two batches.
3   Roll 2 level teaspoons of mixture into ovals; place on trays about 5cm apart. Flatten slightly; use back of fork to roughen surface. Bake about 7 minutes.
4   Meanwhile, make vienna cream.
5   Lift biscuits onto wire rack to cool. Sandwich biscuits with vienna cream and jam.
vienna cream   Beat butter, extract and sifted icing sugar in small bowl with electric mixer until fluffy; beat in milk.

prep and cook time 40 minutes
makes 28

DURING COOKING TIME, SWAP AND ROTATE THE POSITION OF TRAYS OR PANS ON THE OVEN SHELVES – SOME OVENS HAVE HOT SPOTS AND ROTATING THE TRAYS ENSURES EVEN BROWNING.

Lemon madeleines

2 eggs
2 tablespoons caster sugar
2 tablespoons icing sugar
2 teaspoons finely grated lemon rind
¼ cup (35g) self-raising flour
¼ cup (35g) plain flour
75g unsalted butter, melted
1 tablespoon lemon juice
2 tablespoons icing sugar, extra

1 Preheat oven to 200°C/180°C fan-assisted. Grease 12-hole (1½-tablespoons/30ml) madeleine tin (or use a 12-hole bun tin if a madeleine tin is not available).
2 Beat eggs, caster sugar, sifted icing sugar and rind in small bowl with electric mixer until pale and thick.
3 Meanwhile, triple-sift flours; sift flour over egg mixture. Pour butter and juice down the side of the bowl then fold ingredients together. Drop rounded tablespoons of mixture into each hole of tin.
4 Bake madeleines about 10 minutes. Tap hot tin firmly on bench to release onto wire rack to cool. Dust with sifted extra icing sugar.

prep and cook time 25 minutes
makes 12

Flower drops

125g butter, softened
½ teaspoon vanilla extract
½ cup (110g) caster sugar
1 cup (120g) ground almonds
1 egg
1 cup (150g) plain flour
1 teaspoon finely grated lemon rind
⅓ cup (110g) raspberry jam
2 tablespoons apricot jam

1 Preheat oven to 180°C/160°C fan-assisted. Grease oven trays; line with baking parchment.
2 Beat butter, extract, sugar and ground almonds in small bowl with electric mixer until light and fluffy. Beat in egg; stir in sifted flour.
3 Divide rind between both jams; mix well.
4 Roll level tablespoons of mixture into balls; place about 5cm apart on oven trays, flatten slightly. Using end of a wooden spoon, press a flower shape (about 1cm deep) into dough; fill each hole with a little jam, using apricot for centres and raspberry for petals of flowers.
5 Bake drops about 15 minutes. Cool on trays.

prep and cook time 30 minutes
makes 26

Kisses

125g butter
½ cup (110g) caster sugar
1 egg
⅓ cup (50g) plain flour
¼ cup (35g) self-raising flour
⅔ cup (100g) cornflour
¼ cup (30g) custard powder
vienna cream
60g butter
¾ cup (120g) icing sugar
2 teaspoons milk

1   Preheat oven to 200°C/180°C fan-assisted.
2   Beat butter and sugar in small bowl with electric mixer until smooth and creamy; add egg, beat only until combined. Stir in sifted dry ingredients in two batches.
3   Spoon mixture into piping bag fitted with 1cm tube. Pipe mixture into 3cm-diameter rounds, about 3cm apart, onto lightly greased oven trays.

4   Bake kisses about 10 minutes or until browned lightly. Loosen biscuits, cool on trays.
5   Sandwich cold biscuits with vienna cream; dust with a little extra sifted icing sugar, if desired.
vienna cream Beat butter in small bowl with electric mixture until as white as possible. Gradually beat in half the sifted icing sugar, then milk; gradually beat in remaining icing sugar.

prep and cook time 35 minutes
(plus cooling time)
makes 20

A POP-IN-THE-MOUTH,
MELT-IN-THE-MOUTH,
AFTER-DINNER DELIGHT.

Pink macaroons

3 egg whites
2 tablespoons caster sugar
pink food colouring
1¼ cups (200g) icing sugar
1 cup (120g) ground almonds
2 tablespoons icing sugar, extra
white chocolate ganache
100g white eating chocolate, chopped coarsely
2 tablespoons double cream

1 Make white chocolate ganache.

2 Grease oven trays; line with baking parchment.

3 Beat egg whites in small bowl with electric mixer until soft peaks form. Add caster sugar and food colouring, beat until sugar dissolves. Transfer mixture to large bowl; fold in sifted icing sugar and ground almonds, in two batches.

4 Spoon mixture into large piping bag fitted with 1.5cm plain tube. Pipe 36 x 4cm rounds, 2cm apart, onto trays. Tap trays on bench top to help macaroons to spread slightly. Dust with sifted extra icing sugar; stand 15 minutes.

5 Meanwhile, preheat oven to 150°C/130°C fan-assisted.

6 Bake macaroons 20 minutes. Stand on trays 5 minutes; transfer to wire rack to cool.

7 Sandwich macaroons with white chocolate ganache.

white chocolate ganache Stir chocolate and cream in small saucepan over low heat until smooth. Transfer mixture to small bowl. Cover; refrigerate until mixture is spreadable.

prep and cook time 55 minutes
makes 18

Apple crumble custard creams

1 medium apple (150g), peeled, cored, chopped coarsely
2 teaspoons water
125g butter, softened
⅓ cup (75g) firmly packed brown sugar
2 tablespoons apple concentrate
1 cup (150g) self-raising flour
¾ cup (110g) plain flour
¼ cup (30g) oat bran
¼ cup (20g) desiccated coconut
1 teaspoon ground cinnamon
1 tablespoon icing sugar
custard cream
1 tablespoon custard powder
1 tablespoon caster sugar
½ cup (125ml) milk
¼ teaspoon vanilla extract
125g cream cheese, softened

1 Stew apple with the water in small saucepan, covered, over medium heat until tender. Mash with a fork; cool.
2 Beat butter, sugar and concentrate in small bowl with electric mixer until combined. Transfer mixture to medium bowl; stir in sifted flours, oat bran, stewed apple, coconut and cinnamon, in two batches.
3 Knead dough on floured surface until smooth. Roll dough between sheets of baking parchment until 3mm thick; refrigerate 30 minutes.
4 Preheat oven to 180°C/160°C fan-assisted. Grease oven trays; line with baking parchment.
5 Using 6.5cm apple cutter, cut 40 shapes from dough. Place shapes about 3cm apart on oven trays.
6 Bake biscuits about 12 minutes. Cool on wire racks.
7 Meanwhile, make custard cream. Sandwich biscuits with custard cream. Serve dusted with sifted icing sugar.
custard cream Blend custard powder and sugar with milk and extract in small saucepan; stir over heat until mixture boils and thickens. Remove from heat, cover surface with cling film; cool. Beat cream cheese in small bowl with electric mixer until smooth. Add custard; beat until combined.

prep and cook time 42 minutes (plus refrigeration time)
makes 20

Mini Florentines

¾ cup (120g) sultanas
2 cups (80g) corn flakes
¾ cup (60g) flaked almonds, toasted
½ cup (110g) red glacé cherries
⅔ cup (160ml) sweetened condensed milk
60g white eating chocolate, melted
60g dark eating chocolate, melted

QUICK TO MIX AND PRETTY TO PRESENT, THESE GOODIES INSPIRE AN AFTERNOON TEA PLATTER.

1 Preheat oven to 180°C/160°C fan-assisted.
2 Combine sultanas, corn flakes, nuts, cherries and condensed milk in medium bowl.
3 Drop heaped teaspoons of mixture onto baking-parchment-lined oven trays, allowing 5cm between each florentine.
4 Bake florentines for about 6 minutes or until browned lightly. Cool on trays.
5 Spread half of the bases with white chocolate and remaining half with dark chocolate; run fork through chocolate to make waves. Allow chocolate to set at room temperature.

prep and cook time 16 minutes (plus cooling time)
makes 45

Chocolate fudge brownies

150g butter
300g dark eating chocolate, chopped coarsely
1½ cups (330g) firmly packed brown sugar
3 eggs
2 teaspoons vanilla extract
¾ cup (110g) plain flour
¾ cup (140g) dark chocolate chips
½ cup (120g) soured cream
¾ cup (110g) macadamias, toasted, chopped coarsely
1 tablespoon cocoa powder

1   Preheat oven to 180°C/160°C fan-assisted. Grease 19cm x 29cm rectangular baking tin with baking parchment; line base and two long sides with baking parchment, extending paper 2cm above edge of tin.
2   Melt butter in medium saucepan, add chocolate; stir over low heat, without boiling, until mixture is smooth. Stir in sugar, then transfer mixture to large bowl; cool until just warm.
3   Stir in eggs, one at a time, then stir in extract, flour, chocolate chips, cream and nuts. Spread mixture into prepared tin.
4   Bake brownies about 40 minutes. Cover tin with foil, bake further 20 minutes.
5   Cool in tin; turn top-side up onto wire rack, dust with sifted cocoa. Cut into pieces before serving.

prep and cook time 1 hour 25 minutes (plus cooling time)
makes 12

AN AMERICAN CLASSIC, BROWNIES ARE THOUGHT TO HAVE BEEN 'INVENTED' BY ACCIDENT WHEN A NEW ENGLAND HOUSEWIFE FORGOT TO ADD THE BAKING POWDER TO A CHOCOLATE CAKE SHE WAS MAKING. CHOCOLATE LOVERS AROUND THE WORLD HAVE ENJOYED THAT RESULT, IN ONE FORM OR ANOTHER, FOR MORE THAN A CENTURY.

Choc-peppermint slice

250g digestive biscuits
100g butter, chopped
½ cup (125ml) sweetened condensed milk
70g peppermint crisp chocolate, chopped coarsely
chocolate topping
200g milk eating chocolate, chopped coarsely
2 teaspoons vegetable oil

1 Grease 19cm x 29cm baking tin; line base and two long sides with baking parchment, extending paper 2cm over long sides.
2 Process 200g of biscuits until fine; chop remaining biscuits coarsely.
3 Combine butter and milk in small saucepan; stir over low heat until smooth. Combine processed and chopped biscuits with mint chocolate in medium bowl; stir in butter mixture. Press mixture firmly into tin; refrigerate, covered, about 20 minutes or until set.
4 Meanwhile, make chocolate topping. Spread topping over slice. Refrigerate until firm before cutting into 24 squares.
chocolate topping Stir ingredients in small heatproof bowl over saucepan of simmering water, until smooth.

prep and cook time 20 minutes (plus refrigeration time)
makes 24

Variations

lemon Replace peppermint crisp chocolate with 1 teaspoon finely grated lemon rind and 1 tablespoon lemon juice in the biscuit mixture. Press mixture firmly into tin; refrigerate, covered, about 20 minutes or until set. Top with lemon icing made by stirring 1¼ cups (200g) icing sugar with 10g butter and one tablespoon lemon juice in small heatproof bowl over small saucepan of simmering water until smooth.
apricot & coconut Replace peppermint crisp chocolate with ½ cup (40g) toasted shredded coconut and ½ cup (80g) finely chopped dried apricots in the biscuit mixture. Press mixture firmly into tin; refrigerate, covered, about 20 minutes or until set. Top with icing made by stirring 200g coarsely chopped white eating chocolate and 2 teaspoons vegetable oil in small heatproof bowl over small saucepan of simmering water until smooth.
coffee & macadamia Replace peppermint crisp chocolate with ½ cup (70g) coarsely chopped roasted macadamias in the biscuit mixture. Press mixture firmly into tin; refrigerate, covered, about 20 minutes or until set. Top with icing made by dissolving 2 teaspoons instant coffee granules in 2 tablespoons boiling water in small heatproof bowl over small saucepan of simmering water; add 1¼ cups (200g) icing sugar and 10g butter, stirring until smooth.

Left: choc-peppermint slice
Right: lemon slice (top); apricot & coconut slice (middle); coffee & macadamia slice (bottom)

Raspberry coconut slice

90g butter
½ cup (110g) caster sugar
1 egg
¼ cup (35g) self-raising flour
⅔ cup (100g) plain flour
1 tablespoon custard powder
¼ cup (80ml) raspberry jam
coconut topping
2 eggs, beaten lightly
¼ cup (55g) caster sugar
2 cups (180g) desiccated coconut

1 Preheat oven to 180°C/160°C fan-assisted. Grease 19cm x 29cm rectangular baking tin; line base and two long sides with baking parchment, extending paper 2cm above edge of tin.

2 Beat butter, sugar and egg in small bowl with electric mixer until changed to a lighter colour; stir in sifted flours and custard powder.

3 Spread mixture over base of prepared tin.

4 Bake slice 15 minutes. Stand in tin 10 minutes.

5 Spread slice base with jam, sprinkle over coconut topping.

6 Return to oven; bake further 25 minutes or until browned lightly. Cool in tin before cutting.

coconut topping Combine ingredients in medium bowl.

prep and cook time 1 hour 5 minutes (plus cooling time)
makes 12

Caramel coconut slice

½ cup (75g) plain flour
½ cup (75g) self-raising flour
½ cup (45g) desiccated coconut
½ cup (110g) caster sugar
100g butter, melted
caramel filling
395g can sweetened condensed milk
2 tablespoons golden syrup
¼ cup (55g) firmly packed brown sugar
60g butter, melted
coconut topping
4 eggs, beaten lightly
⅔ cup (150g) caster sugar
4 cups (360g) desiccated coconut

1   Preheat oven to 180°C/160°C fan-assisted. Grease 26cm x 32cm swiss roll tin; line base and two long sides with baking parchment, extending paper 2cm above edge of tin.
2   Sift flours into medium bowl, stir in coconut, sugar and butter; press evenly over base of prepared tin.
3   Bake slice about 10 minutes or until lightly browned; cool.
4   Spread caramel filling evenly over base; sprinkle with coconut topping.
5   Return to oven; bake 25 minutes or until topping is browned lightly; cool in tin before cutting.
caramel filling Combine ingredients in bowl; mix well.
coconut topping Combine ingredients in bowl; mix well.

prep and cook time 1 hour
(plus cooling time)
makes 12

Vanilla & passionfruit slice

1 sheet ready-rolled puff pastry, thawed
¼ cup (55g) caster sugar
¼ cup (35g) cornflour
1½ tablespoons custard powder
1¼ cups (310ml) milk
30g butter
1 egg yolk
½ teaspoon vanilla extract
passionfruit icing
¾ cup (110g) icing sugar
1 tablespoon passionfruit pulp
1 teaspoon water, approximately

1 Preheat oven to 240°C/220°C fan-assisted. Grease 8cm x 26cm cake tin; line with strip of foil extending over long sides of tin.
2 Place pastry sheet on oven tray. Bake about 15 minutes or until puffed; cool. Split pastry in half horizontally; remove and discard any uncooked pastry from centre. Flatten pastry pieces gently with hand; trim both to fit tin. Place top half in tin, top-side down.

3 Meanwhile, combine sugar, cornflour and custard powder in medium saucepan; gradually stir in milk. Stir over heat until mixture boils and thickens. Reduce heat; simmer, stirring, about 3 minutes or until custard is thick and smooth. Remove pan from heat; stir in butter, egg yolk and extract.

4 Spread hot custard over pastry in tin; top with remaining pastry, bottom-side up, press down gently. Cool to room temperature.
5 Meanwhile, make passionfruit icing.
6 Spread pastry with icing; set at room temperature. Refrigerate 3 hours before cutting.

passionfruit icing Sift icing sugar into small heatproof bowl; stir in passionfruit and enough water to make a thick paste. Stir over small saucepan of simmering water until icing is spreadable.

prep and cook time 45 minutes
(plus refrigeration time)
makes 12

Apple & rhubarb streusel slice

100g butter, softened
½ cup (110g) caster sugar
1 egg yolk
⅔ cup (100g) plain flour
¼ cup (35g) self-raising flour
1 tablespoon custard powder
4 cups (440g) coarsely chopped rhubarb
2 large granny smith apples (400g), sliced thinly
2 tablespoons honey
1½ teaspoons finely grated orange rind
streusel topping
½ cup (75g) plain flour
¼ cup (35g) self-raising flour
⅓ cup (75g) firmly packed brown sugar
½ teaspoon ground cinnamon
80g butter, chopped coarsely

1 Make streusel topping.

2 Preheat oven to 180°C/160°C fan-assisted. Line 20cm x 30cm baking tin with baking parchment, extending the paper 2cm over long sides.

3 Beat butter, sugar and yolk in small bowl with electric mixer until light and fluffy. Stir in sifted flours and custard powder. Press mixture over base of tin.

4 Bake base for about 20 minutes or until browned lightly. Cool 15 minutes.

5 Increase oven to 200°C/180°C fan-assisted.

6 Meanwhile, cook rhubarb, apple, honey and rind in medium saucepan, stirring occasionally, about 5 minutes or until apples are just tender; cool 15 minutes.

7 Spread rhubarb mixture over base; coarsely grate streusel over fruit.

8 Bake slice about 15 minutes. Cool in tin before cutting.

streusel topping Blend or process flours, sugar and cinnamon until combined. Add butter; process until ingredients come together. Enclose in cling film; freeze 1 hour.

prep and cook time 1 hour 5 minutes (plus cooling and freezing times)
makes 15

Mincemeat slice

90g butter, softened
⅓ cup (75g) firmly packed brown sugar
1 cup (150g) plain flour
topping
1 cup (340g) mincemeat
2 eggs
½ cup (110g) firmly packed brown sugar
2 tablespoons brandy
1 tablespoon self-raising flour
1½ cups (120g) desiccated coconut

1 Preheat oven to 180°C/160°C fan-assisted. Grease 20cm x 30cm baking tin; line with baking parchment, extending paper 2cm over long sides.
2 Beat butter and sugar in small bowl with electric mixer until pale in colour; stir in sifted flour, in two batches. Press dough over base of tin. Bake 10 minutes.
3 Meanwhile, make topping. Press topping gently over base.
4 Bake slice about 25 minutes or until golden brown. Cool in tin before cutting.
topping Blend or process mincemeat until chopped finely. Beat eggs, sugar and brandy in small bowl with electric mixer until thick and creamy; stir in flour, coconut and mince.

prep and cook time 45 minutes
makes 60

MINCEMEAT CAN BE BOUGHT THROUGHOUT THE YEAR, OR JUST MAYBE, YOU HAVE SOME HOME-MADE MINCEMEAT LEFTOVER FROM CHRISTMAS. BOTH WILL WORK WELL IN THIS RECIPE. SERVE THE SLICE CUT INTO SMALL BARS – IT'S VERY RICH.

Little Cakes

APPLE GINGER CAKES
drizzled with icing

HOT CROSS BUNS

decadent
BLACKFOREST CAKES

Clever cupcakes

IT'S NOT SO LONG AGO THAT LITTLE CAKES WERE CONSIDERED KID'S PARTY FARE, BUT IN RECENT YEARS THEY'VE GROWN UP AND BECOME QUITE SOPHISTICATED

Gingerbread loaves

200g butter, softened
1¼ cups (275g) caster sugar
¾ cup (270g) treacle
2 eggs
3 cups (450g) plain flour
1½ tablespoons ground ginger
3 teaspoons mixed spice
1 teaspoon bicarbonate of soda
¾ cup (180ml) milk
vanilla icing
3 cups (500g) icing sugar
2 teaspoons butter, softened
½ teaspoon vanilla extract
⅓ cup (80ml) milk

1 Preheat oven to 200°C/180°C fan-assisted. Grease two eight-hole (½-cup/125ml) mini loaf trays or line two muffin trays (⅓-cup/80ml) with paper cases.

2 Beat butter and sugar in small bowl with electric mixer until light and fluffy. Pour in treacle, beat for 3 minutes. Add eggs one at a time, beating until just combined after each addition. Transfer mixture to large bowl. Stir in sifted dry ingredients, then milk. Divide mixture among prepared trays.

3 Bake loaves about 25 minutes. Stand 5 minutes before turning out onto wire rack to cool.

4 Spread icing over loaves; stand until set.

vanilla icing Sift icing sugar into heatproof bowl; stir in butter, vanilla and milk to form a smooth paste. Place bowl over simmering water; stir until icing is a spreadable consistency.

prep and cook time 1 hour
(plus cooling time)
makes 16

DARK, THICK, STICKY
TREACLE AND GINGER
ARE OLD FRIENDS.

Coffee caramel cakes

125g butter, softened
²/₃ cup (150g) firmly packed brown sugar
2 tablespoons instant coffee powder
1 tablespoon boiling water
2 eggs
2 cups (300g) self-raising flour
½ cup (125ml) milk
18 (130g) soft caramels, halved

1 Preheat oven to 200°C/180°C fan-assisted. Grease 12-hole (⅓-cup/80ml) muffin tray.
2 Beat butter and sugar in small bowl with electric mixer until light and fluffy. Add combined coffee and the water, then beat in eggs, one at a time, beating until just combined between additions. Transfer mixture to large bowl.
3 Stir in sifted flour and milk. Spoon mixture into prepared tray. Press 3 caramel halves into the centre of each cake; cover with batter.
4 Bake cakes about 20 minutes. Cool in tray 5 minutes; turn cakes onto wire racks to cool..

prep and cook time 35 minutes
(plus cooling time)
makes 12

Banana blueberry cakes

125g butter
½ cup (125ml) milk
2 eggs
1 cup (220g) caster sugar
½ cup mashed banana
1½ cups (225g) self-raising flour
½ cup (75g) frozen blueberries

1 Preheat oven to 200°C/180°C fan-assisted. Grease 12-hole (⅓-cup/ 80ml) muffin tray.
2 Place butter and milk in small saucepan; stir over low heat until butter melts.
3 Beat eggs in small bowl with electric mixer until thick and creamy. Gradually add sugar, beating until dissolved between additions; stir in banana. Fold in sifted flour and cooled butter mixture, in two batches. Divide mixture among muffin tray.
4 Bake cakes 10 minutes. Remove tray from oven; press frozen blueberries into tops of cakes. Return to oven, bake further 15 minutes. Turn cakes onto wire racks to cool.

prep and cook time 50 minutes (plus cooling time)
makes 12

YOU WILL NEED ONE LARGE (230G) OVERRIPE BANANA FOR THIS RECIPE.

Black forest cakes

425g can pitted cherries in syrup
165g butter, chopped coarsely
100g dark eating chocolate, chopped coarsely
1⅓ cups (295g) caster sugar
¼ cup (60ml) cherry brandy
1 cup (150g) plain flour
2 tablespoons self-raising flour
2 tablespoons cocoa powder
1 egg
⅔ cup (160ml) whipping cream, whipped
2 teaspoons cherry brandy, extra
100g dark eating chocolate, extra

1   Preheat oven to 160°C/140°C fan-assisted. Line 12-hole (⅓-cup/80ml) muffin tray with paper cases.
2   Drain cherries; reserve syrup. Process ½ cup (110g) cherries with ½ cup (125ml) of the syrup until smooth. Halve remaining cherries; reserve for decorating cakes. Discard remaining syrup.
3   Stir butter, chocolate, sugar, brandy and cherry puree in small saucepan over low heat until chocolate is melted. Transfer mixture to medium bowl; cool 15 minutes. Whisk in sifted flours and cocoa, then egg. Divide mixture among cases; smooth surface.
4   Bake cakes about 40 minutes. Turn cakes, top-side up, onto wire racks to cool.
5   Top cakes with remaining cherries and combined cream and extra brandy. Using a vegetable peeler, make small chocolate curls from extra chocolate; sprinkle over cakes.

prep and cook time 1 hour 5 minutes (plus cooling time)
makes 12

USING A VEGETABLE PEELER TO MAKE CUTE LITTLE CHOCOLATE CURLS IS A QUICK AND EASY WAY TO DRESS UP CAKES.

Apple ginger cakes with lemon icing

250g butter, softened
1½ cups (330g) firmly packed dark brown sugar
3 eggs
¼ cup (90g) golden syrup
2 cups (300g) plain flour
1½ teaspoons bicarbonate of soda
2 tablespoons ground ginger
1 tablespoon ground cinnamon
1 cup (170g) coarsely grated apple
⅔ cup (160ml) hot water
lemon icing
2 cups (320g) icing sugar
2 teaspoons butter, softened
⅓ cup (80ml) lemon juice

1   Preheat oven to moderate. Grease two six-hole mini fluted tube pans or texas muffin pans.
2   Beat butter and sugar in small bowl with electric mixer until light and fluffy. Add eggs, one at a time, beat until well combined between additions. Stir in syrup.
3   Transfer mixture to medium bowl; stir in sifted dry ingredients, then apple and the water.
4   Divide mixture among prepared pans, smooth tops.
5   Bake in moderate oven about 25 minutes. Stand cakes in pan 5 minutes then turn onto wire racks to cool.
6   Drizzle lemon icing over cakes.
lemon icing Sift icing sugar into medium heatproof bowl; stir in butter and juice to form a paste. Place bowl over small saucepan of simmering water; stir until icing is a pouring consistency.

prep and cook time 40 minutes (plus cooling time)
makes 12

IT'S THE FABULOUS FUSION OF FLAVOURS THAT MAKES THESE LITTLE CAKES UNIQUE. YOU WILL NEED ONE LARGE APPLE (200G) FOR THIS RECIPE.

Buttery apple cinnamon cakes

125g butter, softened
1 teaspoon vanilla extract
¾ cup (165g) caster sugar
2 eggs
¾ cup (110g) self-raising flour
¼ cup (35g) plain flour
⅓ cup (80ml) apple juice
1 small red apple (130g)
1½ tablespoons demerara sugar
¼ teaspoon ground cinnamon

1 Preheat oven to 200°C/180°C fan-assisted. Grease an eight-hole (½-cup/125ml) mini loaf tray (the mixture can also be cooked in a large muffin tray).
2 Beat butter, extract and sugar in small bowl with electric mixer until light and fluffy. Add eggs, one at a time, beating until just combined between additions.
3 Fold in combined sifted flours and juice in two batches. Spread mixture into prepared tray.
4 Cut the unpeeled apple into quarters; remove core, slice thinly. Overlap apple slices on top of cakes.
5 Combine demerara sugar and cinnamon in small bowl; sprinkle half the sugar mixture over cakes.
6 Bake cakes about 25 minutes. Turn onto wire rack to cool. Sprinkle with remaining sugar mixture.

prep and cook time 35 minutes (plus cooling time)
makes 8

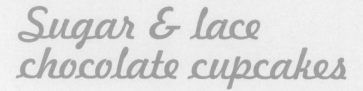

Sugar & lace chocolate cupcakes

125g butter, chopped coarsely
100g white eating chocolate, chopped coarsely
²⁄₃ cup (150g) firmly packed brown sugar
¼ cup (90g) golden syrup
²⁄₃ cup (160ml) milk
1 cup (150g) plain flour
¹⁄₃ cup (50g) self-raising flour
1 egg
doily, lace or stencil
½ cup (80g) icing sugar

1   Preheat oven to 160°C/140°C fan-assisted. Line 6-hole large (¾-cup/180ml) muffin tray with paper cases.
2   Combine butter, chocolate, brown sugar, syrup and milk in small saucepan; stir over low heat, until smooth. Transfer mixture to medium bowl; cool 15 minutes. Whisk sifted flours into chocolate mixture, then egg. Divide mixture among cases.
3   Bake cakes about 40 minutes. Turn cakes, top-side up, onto wire rack to cool.
4   Place doily, lace or stencil over cake; sift a little icing sugar over doily, then carefully lift doily from cake. Repeat with remaining cakes and icing sugar.

prep and cook time 1 hour (plus cooling time)
makes 6

SIFTING ICING SUGAR OVER A DOILY, STENCIL OR A PIECE OF LACE SOUNDS EASIER THAN IT IS. YOU NEED A DEFINED CLEAR DESIGN TO KEEP THE PATTERN CREATED BY THE ICING SUGAR ONCE THE DOILY IS LIFTED AWAY. IF THE DOILY HAS A SMALL PATTERN, USE SOME SHARP SCISSORS TO CUT PIECES AWAY TO ENLARGE THE DESIGN.

Banoffee cupcakes

90g butter, softened
½ cup (110g) firmly packed brown sugar
2 eggs
½ cup (75g) plain flour
½ cup (75g) self-raising flour
½ teaspoon bicarbonate of soda
½ teaspoon mixed spice
⅔ cup mashed banana
⅓ cup (80g) soured cream
2 tablespoons milk
380g dulce de leche
½ cup (125ml) whipping cream, whipped
2 medium bananas (400g), sliced thinly
100g dark eating chocolate

1   Preheat oven to 180°C/160°C fan-assisted. Line 6-hole large (¾-cup/180ml) muffin tray with paper cases.
2   Beat butter, sugar and eggs in small bowl with electric mixer until light and fluffy. Stir in sifted dry ingredients, banana, soured cream and milk. Divide mixture among cases; smooth surface.
3   Bake cakes about 25 minutes. Turn cakes, top-side up, onto wire rack to cool. Remove paper cases from cakes.
4   Fold 2 tablespoons of the dulce de leche into cream. Split cakes into three layers. Re-assemble cakes with remaining caramel and banana. Top cakes with caramel cream. Using a vegetable peeler, make small curls from the chocolate; sprinkle over cakes.

prep and cook time 45 minutes
makes 6

Hot cross buns

2 x 7g sachets granulated yeast
¼ cup (55g) caster sugar
1½ cups (375ml) warm milk
4 cups (600g) plain flour
1 teaspoon mixed spice
½ teaspoon ground cinnamon
60g butter
1 egg
¾ cup (120g) sultanas
flour paste for crosses
½ cup (75g) plain flour
2 teaspoons caster sugar
⅓ cup (80ml) water, approximately
glaze
1 tablespoon caster sugar
1 teaspoon gelatine
1 tablespoon water

1   Combine yeast, sugar and milk in small bowl or jug; cover, stand in warm place about 10 minutes or until mixture is frothy.

2   Sift flour and spices into large bowl, rub in butter. Stir in yeast mixture, egg and sultanas; mix to a soft sticky dough. Cover; stand in warm place about 45 minutes or until dough has doubled in size.

3   Grease 23cm-square shallow cake tin.

4   Turn dough onto floured surface, knead about 5 minutes or until smooth. Divide dough into 16 pieces, knead into balls. Place balls into prepared tin; cover, stand in warm place about 10 minutes or until buns have risen to top of tin.

5   Meanwhile, preheat oven to 220°C/200°C fan-assisted.

6   Place flour paste for crosses in piping bag fitted with small plain tube, pipe crosses on buns.

7   Bake buns about 20 minutes or until well browned. Turn buns onto wire rack, brush tops with hot glaze; cool on wire rack.

flour paste for crosses   Combine flour and sugar in bowl. Gradually blend in enough of the water to form a smooth paste.

glaze   Combine ingredients in small saucepan; stir over heat, without boiling, until sugar and gelatine are dissolved.

prep and cook time 1 hour 25 minutes
(plus standing and cooling time)
makes 16

ALTHOUGH THESE DELICIOUS EASTER TREATS ARE NOW SERVED ON GOOD FRIDAY, IN OLDEN TIMES THEY WERE THOUGHT TO HAVE HOLY POWERS AND WERE PRESENT IN MANY RELIGIOUS OBSERVANCES.

Big Cakes

BEST EVER SPONGE

super-moist
RICH FRUIT CAKE

CHOCOLATE CAKE
with fudge frosting

Tiramisu torte

WHETHER IT IS SERVED AS A
TEATIME TREAT, A DECADENT
DESSERT OR A PARTY CENTREPIECE,
NOTHING CAN BEAT A SLICE OF
HOME MADE CAKE

Citrus polenta cake

¾ cup (165g) caster sugar
1¼ cups (310ml) water
1 medium unpeeled orange (240g), sliced thinly
1 large unpeeled lemon (180g), sliced thinly
¼ cup (60ml) water, extra
125g butter, softened
1 tablespoon finely grated lemon rind
1 cup (220g) caster sugar, extra
3 eggs
½ cup (60g) ground almonds
½ cup (75g) plain flour
½ cup (75g) self-raising flour
¾ cup (120g) polenta
⅓ cup (80g) soured cream
¼ cup (60ml) lemon juice
lemon mascarpone
1 cup (250g) mascarpone cheese
2 teaspoons finely grated lemon rind
1 tablespoon lemon juice
2 tablespoons caster sugar

1   Preheat oven to 180°C/160°C fan-assisted. Grease deep 20cm-round cake tin; line base and side with baking parchment.
2   Combine sugar and the water in large frying pan; using wooden spoon, stir over heat, without boiling, until sugar dissolves. Bring to a boil, reduce heat; simmer, without stirring, uncovered, about 5 minutes or until syrup thickens slightly. Add orange and lemon slices; simmer gently, uncovered, about 7 minutes or until rind is tender, turning slices halfway through cooking time.
3   Remove syrup mixture from heat. Using tongs, lift alternate orange and lemon slices directly from syrup to cover base and side of prepared tin. Reserve syrup.
4   Add the extra water to reserved syrup in pan; bring to a boil. Reduce heat; simmer, uncovered, without stirring, about 5 minutes or until syrup is a light honey colour. Pour hot syrup over orange and lemon slices.
5   Beat butter, rind and extra sugar in small bowl with electric mixer until light and fluffy. Beat in eggs, one at a time, until combined. (Mixture will curdle, but will come together later.)
6   Transfer mixture to large bowl; using wooden spoon, stir in ground almonds, flours, polenta, soured cream and juice. Carefully spread mixture into prepared tin.
7   Bake cake about 1¼ hours. Stand cake in tin 15 minutes before turning onto serving plate. Serve cake warm with lemon mascarpone.
lemon mascarpone   Combine ingredients in small bowl; whisk until smooth.

prep and cook time 2 hours 5 minutes (plus standing time)
serves 12

Buttery orange cake

250g butter, softened
2 tablespoons finely grated orange rind
1½ cups (330g) caster sugar
4 eggs
1½ cups (225g) self-raising flour
½ cup (75g) plain flour
¾ cup (180ml) orange juice
glacé icing
1½ cups (240g) icing sugar
1 teaspoon soft butter
2 tablespoons orange juice

1   Preheat oven to 160°C/140°C fan-assisted. Grease deep 22cm-round cake tin; line base and side with baking parchment, bringing paper 5cm above edge of tin.

2   Beat butter, rind and sugar in large bowl with electric mixer until light and fluffy. Add eggs, one at a time, beating until just combined between additions. Fold in combined sifted flours and juice in two batches. Spread mixture into prepared tin.

3   Bake cake about 1 hour. Stand cake in tin 5 minutes before turning out onto wire rack to cool.

glacé icing   Sift icing sugar into small heatproof bowl; stir in butter and juice to form a firm paste. Place bowl over small saucepan of simmering water, stir until icing is a spreadable consistency; do not overheat. Top cake with glacé icing.

prep and cook time 1 hour 20 minutes (plus cooling time)
serves 12

Cut & keep butter cake

125g butter, softened
1 teaspoon vanilla extract
1¼ cups (275g) caster sugar
3 eggs
1 cup (150g) plain flour
½ cup (75g) self-raising flour
¼ teaspoon bicarbonate of soda
½ cup (125ml) milk

1   Preheat oven to 160°C/140°C fan-assisted. Grease deep 20cm-round cake tin; line base with baking parchment.
2   Beat ingredients in medium bowl on low speed with electric mixer until just combined. Increase speed to medium; beat until mixture is smooth and changed to a paler colour. Pour mixture into prepared tin.
3   Bake cake about 1¼ hours. Stand cake in tin 5 minutes before turning onto wire rack; turn cake top-side up to cool. Dust cake with sifted icing sugar, if desired.

prep and cook time 1 hour 30 minutes (plus cooling time)
serves 10

THIS IS AN EASY-TO-MIX, ONE-BOWL, PLAIN CAKE – AND THERE'S NOTHING NICER WITH A CUPPA. SIMPLY DUST IT WITH SIFTED ICING SUGAR WHEN SERVING.

Super-moist rich fruit cake

2¼ cups (380g) raisins, chopped coarsely
3 cups (480g) sultanas
¾ cup (110g) currants
1 cup (250g) quartered red glacé cherries
1½ cups (250g) coarsely chopped pitted prunes
⅓ cup (120g) honey
½ cup (125ml) brandy
250g butter, softened
1 cup (220g) firmly packed black sugar
5 eggs
1¼ cups (185g) plain flour
2 tablespoons brandy, extra

1 Combine fruit, honey and brandy in large bowl; cover; stand overnight.
2 Preheat oven to 150°C/130°C fan-assisted. Line base and sides of deep 19cm-square cake tin with three thicknesses baking parchment, bringing paper 5cm above sides of tin.
3 Beat butter and sugar in small bowl with electric mixer until just combined; beat in eggs, one at a time, until just combined between additions. (The mixture may curdle at this point, but will come together later.)
4 Add butter mixture to fruit mixture with flour; mix thoroughly with one hand.
5 Drop dollops of mixture into corners of prepared tin to hold baking parchment in position; spread remaining mixture into tin.
6 Drop cake tin from a height of about 15cm onto worktop to settle mixture into tin and to break any large air bubbles; level surface of cake mixture with wet metal spatula.
7 Bake cake about 4 hours. (Cover cake loosely with foil during baking if it starts to overbrown. Give the cake quarter turns several times during baking to avoid it browning unevenly.)
8 Remove cake from oven, brush with extra brandy. Cover tin tightly with foil; cool cake in tin.

prep and cook time 4 hours 30 minutes
(plus standing and cooling time)
serves 36

THIS CAKE IS EXTREMELY MOIST, DUE TO THE PROPORTION OF FRUIT TO FLOUR, WHICH GIVES IT A SIMILAR TEXTURE TO CHRISTMAS PUDDING. GREAT AS A FAMILY DESSERT WITH CUSTARD OR, TRADITIONALLY, FOR MORE SPECIAL OCCASIONS SUCH AS BIRTHDAYS AND WEDDINGS.

Last-minute Christmas cake

1kg mixed dried fruit
½ cup (100g) glacé cherries, halved
250g butter, chopped
1 cup (200g) firmly packed brown sugar
1 cup (250ml) fortified dessert wine
1 cup (150g) coarsely chopped brazil nuts
1 tablespoon finely grated orange rind
1 tablespoon treacle
5 eggs, beaten lightly
1¾ cups (260g) plain flour
⅓ cup (50g) self-raising flour
½ teaspoon bicarbonate of soda
1 cup (150g) brazil nuts, extra
¼ cup (60ml) fortified dessert wine, extra

1 Combine fruit, butter, sugar and wine in large saucepan; stir over low heat until butter is melted and sugar dissolved. Bring to a boil; remove from heat. Transfer to large bowl; cool.
2 Preheat oven to 150°C/130°C fan-assisted. Line base and sides of deep 23cm-square cake tin with two layers brown paper and two layers baking parchment, bringing paper 5cm above sides of tin.
3 Stir nuts, rind, treacle and eggs into fruit mixture, then add sifted dry ingredients. Spread mixture into prepared tin; place extra nuts on top.
4 Bake cake about 2½ hours or until cooked when tested. Brush top of cake with extra wine, cover hot cake tightly with foil; cool in tin.

prep and cook time 3 hours 5 minutes (plus cooling time)
serves 30

Egg-free date & nut cake

1 cup (360g) honey
1 cup (250ml) water
30g butter
2¼ cups (360g) wholemeal self-raising flour
1 teaspoon mixed spice
½ teaspoon ground ginger
1½ cups (250g) pitted chopped dates
¾ cup (90g) chopped walnuts
¼ cup (35g) chopped slivered almonds

A SLICE OF THIS HEARTY, HEALTHY CAKE IS A DECENT BREAKFAST ON THE RUN OR A RELIABLE MID-MORNING PICK-ME-UP.

1 Preheat oven to 180°C/160°C fan-assisted. Grease deep 19cm-square cake tin; line base with baking parchment.
2 Combine honey, water and butter in medium saucepan, stir over low heat until butter melts.
3 Combine sifted flour and spices, dates and nuts in medium bowl; stir in warm honey mixture. Spread cake mixture into prepared tin.
4 Bake cake about 40 minutes. Stand cake in tin 5 minutes before turning onto wire rack to cool. Glaze with a little extra honey, if desired.

Prep and cook time 55 minutes
(plus cooling time)
serves 9

Orange poppy seed syrup cake

⅓ cup (50g) poppy seeds
¼ cup (60ml) milk
185g butter, softened
1 tablespoon finely grated orange rind
1 cup (220g) caster sugar
3 eggs
1½ cups (225g) self-raising flour
½ cup (75g) plain flour
½ cup (60g) ground almonds
½ cup (125ml) orange juice
orange syrup
1 cup (220g) caster sugar
⅔ cup (160ml) orange juice
⅓ cup (80ml) water

1   Preheat oven to 180°C/160°C fan-assisted. Grease deep 22cm-round cake tin; line base and side with baking parchment.
2   Combine seeds and milk in small bowl; stand 20 minutes.
3   Meanwhile, beat butter, rind and sugar in small bowl with electric mixer until light and fluffy; beat in eggs, one at a time, until just combined between additions.
4   Transfer mixture to large bowl; using wooden spoon, stir in flours, ground almonds, juice and poppy-seed mixture. Spread mixture into prepared tin.
5   Bake cake about 1 hour. Stand cake in tin 5 minutes before turning onto wire rack over tray; turn top-side up, pour hot syrup over hot cake. Return any syrup that drips onto tray to jug; pour over cake.
orange syrup   Using wooden spoon, stir combined ingredients in small saucepan over heat, without boiling, until sugar dissolves. Bring to a boil; reduce heat. Simmer, uncovered, without stirring, 2 minutes. Pour syrup into heatproof jug.

prep and cook time 1 hour 25 minutes (plus standing time)
serves 16

A POPULAR COMBINATION OF FLAVOURS MAKES
THIS SYRUPY CAKE A DEFINITE FAVOURITE.
IF YOU PREFER TO OMIT THE SYRUP COMPLETELY,
THE CAKE ITSELF IS STILL DELICIOUSLY MOIST.

Best-ever sponge cake

4 eggs
¾ cup (165g) caster sugar
1 cup (150g) self-raising flour
1 tablespoon cornflour
10g butter, softened
⅓ cup (80ml) hot water
⅓ cup (110g) lemon curd
¾ cup (180ml) whipping cream, whipped
1 tablespoon icing sugar

1 Preheat oven to 180°C/160°C fan-assisted. Grease two deep 20cm-round cake tins.

2 Beat eggs in large bowl with electric mixer until thick and foamy. Gradually add sugar, about a tablespoon at a time, beating until sugar is dissolved between additions. Total beating time should be about 10 minutes.

3 Sift flour and cornflour together three times onto baking parchment. Sift flour mixture over egg mixture; using one hand like a rake, quickly and lightly fold and pull flour mixture through egg mixture, using the side of your hand as a scraper to make sure all the ingredients are combined.

4 Pour combined butter and the water down side of bowl; using one hand, fold through egg mixture. Pour mixture evenly into prepared tins; using metal spatula, spread mixture to edges of tins.

5 Bake sponges about 25 minutes. Immediately sponges are baked, turn onto wire racks covered with baking parchment; turn top-side up to cool.

6 Place one sponge on serving plate, spread with lemon curd and whipped cream. Top with remaining cake, dust with sifted icing sugar.

prep and cook time 50 minutes (plus cooling time)
serves 8

Low-fat chocolate cake

½ cup (160g) plum jam
½ cup (110g) firmly packed brown sugar
½ cup (50g) cocoa powder
¾ cup (180ml) low fat evaporated milk
2 teaspoons dry instant coffee
50g butter
2 eggs
½ cup (110g) caster sugar
1 cup (150g) self-raising flour
⅓ cup (50g) plain flour
2 teaspoons icing sugar

1 Preheat oven to 180°C/160°C fan-assisted. Spray 21cm baba cake tin with cooking-oil spray.
2 Combine jam, brown sugar, sifted cocoa, milk, coffee and butter in medium saucepan. Stir over low heat until butter is melted and mixture is smooth (do not boil). Cool.
3 Beat eggs and caster sugar in small bowl with electric mixer until thick and pale. Transfer mixture to large bowl. Stir in sifted flours and chocolate mixture. Pour mixture into prepared tin.
4 Bake cake about 45 minutes. Stand cake in tin 5 minutes before turning onto wire rack to cool.
5 Serve cake dusted with sifted icing, if desired.

prep and cook time 1 hour 5 minutes (plus cooling time)
serves 12

Plum & hazelnut upside-down cake

50g butter, chopped
½ cup (110g) firmly packed brown sugar
6 medium plums (680g), halved, stones removed
185g butter, softened, extra
1 cup (220g) firmly packed brown sugar, extra
3 eggs
½ cup (50g) ground hazelnuts
½ cup (75g) self-raising flour
½ cup (75g) plain flour

1 Preheat oven to 180°C/160°C fan-assisted. Grease deep 22cm-round cake tin; line base with baking parchment.
2 Combine butter and sugar in small saucepan, stir over low heat until smooth; pour over cake tin base. Place plums, cut side down, over tin base.
3 Beat extra butter and extra sugar in small bowl with electric mixer until creamy. Add eggs, one at a time, beating until combined between additions; transfer mixture to large bowl.
4 Stir in ground hazelnuts and sifted flours; spread mixture into prepared tin.
5 Bake cake about 1 hour. Stand cake in tin 5 minutes before turning onto serving plate.

prep and cook time 1 hour 15 minutes
serves 8

Glacé peach & almond cake

185g butter, softened
½ teaspoon almond essence
¾ cup (165g) caster sugar
3 eggs
1 cup (250g) finely chopped glacé peaches
⅓ cup (40g) ground almonds
1½ cups (225g) self-raising flour
½ cup (75g) plain flour
½ cup (125ml) milk
2 tablespoons brandy

1 Preheat oven to 180°C/160°C fan-assisted. Grease 21cm baba cake tin.
2 Beat butter, essence and sugar in medium bowl with electric mixer until light and fluffy. Beat in eggs, one at a time, beating until just combined between additions.
3 Transfer mixture to large bowl; stir in peaches, ground almonds, sifted flours, milk and brandy, in two batches. Spread cake mixture into prepared tin.
4 Bake cake about 1 hour. Stand cake in tin 5 minutes before turning top-side up onto wire rack to cool.

prep and cook time 1 hour 20 minutes (plus cooling time)
serves 6

Family chocolate cake

2 cups (500ml) water
3 cups (660g) caster sugar
250g butter, chopped
⅓ cup (35g) cocoa powder
1 teaspoon bicarbonate of soda
3 cups (450g) self-raising flour
4 eggs, beaten lightly
fudge frosting
90g butter
⅓ cup (80ml) water
½ cup (110g) caster sugar
1½ cups (240g) icing sugar
⅓ cup (35g) cocoa powder

1 Preheat oven to 180°C/160°C fan-assisted. Grease deep 26.5cm x 33cm (14-cup/3.5-litre) baking dish; line base with baking parchment.
2 Combine the water, sugar, butter and combined sifted cocoa and soda in medium saucepan; stir over heat, without boiling, until sugar dissolves. Bring to a boil then reduce heat; simmer, uncovered, 5 minutes. Transfer mixture to large bowl; cool to room temperature.
3 Add flour and egg to bowl; beat with electric mixer until mixture is smooth and changed to a paler colour. Pour mixture into prepared baking dish.
4 Bake cake about 50 minutes. Stand cake in dish 5 minutes before turning onto wire rack; turn cake top-side up to cool.
5 Spread cold cake with fudge frosting.
fudge frosting Combine butter, the water and caster sugar in small saucepan; stir over heat, without boiling, until sugar dissolves. Sift icing sugar and cocoa into small bowl then gradually stir in hot butter mixture. Cover; refrigerate about 20 minutes or until frosting thickens. Beat with wooden spoon until spreadable.

prep and cook time 1 hour 20 minutes (plus cooling and refrigeration time)
serves 20

White chocolate mud cake

250g butter, chopped coarsely
150g white eating chocolate, chopped coarsely
2 cups (440g) caster sugar
1 cup (250ml) milk
1½ cups (225g) plain flour
½ cup (75g) self-raising flour
1 teaspoon vanilla extract
2 eggs, beaten lightly
white chocolate ganache
½ cup (125ml) double cream
300g white eating chocolate, chopped coarsely

1 Preheat oven to 160°C/140°C fan-assisted. Grease deep 20cm-round cake tin; line base and side with baking parchment.
2 Combine butter, chocolate, sugar and milk in medium saucepan; using wooden spoon, stir over low heat, without boiling, until smooth. Transfer mixture to large bowl; cool 15 minutes.
3 Whisk in flours then extract and egg; pour mixture into prepared tin.
4 Bake cake 1 hour. Cover tin loosely with foil; bake further 1 hour. Discard foil, stand cake in tin 5 minutes before turning onto wire rack; turn top-side up to cool.
5 Place cake on serving plate, spread all over with white chocolate ganache. Decorate with chocolate curls, if desired.
white chocolate ganache Bring cream to a boil in small saucepan; pour over chocolate in small bowl, stir with wooden spoon until chocolate melts. Cover bowl; refrigerate, stirring occasionally, about 30 minutes or until ganache is of a spreadable consistency.

prep and cook time 2 hour 40 minutes (plus cooling and refrigeration time)
serves 12

THE WHITE CHOCOLATE MUD CAKE HAS RAPIDLY ASCENDED THE LADDER TO THE TOP OF THE SPECIAL-OCCASION FAVOURITE-CAKE LIST

Raspberry & almond mascarpone cake

500g butter, softened
3 cups (660g) caster sugar
8 eggs
2 cups (300g) plain flour
1½ cups (225g) self-raising flour
1 cup (125g) ground almonds
1 cup (250ml) milk
1 cup (140g) slivered almonds, toasted, chopped finely
400g fresh or frozen raspberries
400g caramelised almonds
mascarpone cream
750g mascarpone cheese
300g soured cream
1 cup (160g) icing sugar
⅓ cup (80ml) Cointreau or Grand Marnier

1 Preheat oven to 160°C/140°C fan-assisted. Grease deep 30cm-round cake tin; line base and sides with two layers of baking parchment, extending 5cm above edge of tin.
2 Beat butter and sugar in large bowl with electric mixer until light and fluffy. Add eggs one at a time, beating until just combined between additions (the mixture may appear curdled at this stage).
3 Transfer mixture to very large bowl; fold in sifted flours, ground almonds and milk in three batches. Fold in chopped almonds and raspberries, then spread mixture into prepared tin.
4 Bake cake 1 hour, then reduce oven temperature to 150°C/130°C fan-assisted and bake about 1 hour. Stand cake in tin 20 minutes before turning onto wire rack to cool.
5 Using large serrated knife, split cake into three layers. Place base layer on serving plate; spread with a third of the mascarpone cream, repeat layering, ending with mascarpone cream. Decorate top of cake with caramelised almonds.
mascarpone cream Beat mascarpone, soured cream and icing sugar in large bowl with electric mixer until soft peaks form; stir in liqueur.

prep and cook time 2 hour 45 minutes
(plus standing and cooling time)
serves 25

Mississippi mud cake

250g butter, chopped coarsely
150g dark eating chocolate, chopped coarsely
2 cups (440g) caster sugar
1 cup (250ml) hot water
⅓ cup (80ml) coffee liqueur
1 tablespoon instant coffee powder
1½ cups (225g) plain flour
¼ cup (35g) self-raising flour
¼ cup (25g) cocoa powder
2 eggs, beaten lightly

1   Preheat oven to 160°C/140°C fan-assisted. Grease deep 20cm-round cake tin; line base and sides with baking parchment.
2   Combine butter, chocolate, sugar, the water, liqueur and coffee powder in medium saucepan. Using wooden spoon, stir over low heat until chocolate melts.
3   Transfer mixture to large bowl; cool 15 minutes. Whisk in combined sifted flours and cocoa, then eggs. Pour mixture into prepared tin.
4   Bake cake about 1½ hours. (Cover cake loosely with foil during baking if it starts to overbrown.)
5   Stand cake in tin 30 minutes before turning onto wire rack; turn cake top-side up to cool. Dust with sifted cocoa, if desired.

prep and cook time 2 hours
(plus cooling and standing time)
serves 16

THIS POPULAR CAKE IS A
DELECTABLE ALTERNATIVE TO
FRUIT CAKE FOR WEDDINGS
AND OTHER OCCASIONS.
IT IS ALSO WONDERFUL
AFTER DINNER WITH COFFEE,
SERVED WARM OR AT ROOM
TEMPERATURE WITH WHIPPED
CREAM AND BERRIES.

Tiramisu torte

6 eggs
1 cup (220g) caster sugar
½ cup (75g) plain flour
½ cup (75g) self-raising flour
½ cup (75g) cornflour
¼ cup (10g) instant coffee powder
1½ cups (375ml) boiling water
¾ cup (180ml) marsala
¼ cup (60ml) coffee-flavoured liqueur
300ml whipping cream
½ cup (80g) icing sugar
750g mascarpone cheese
500g caramelised almonds, chopped coarsely

1 Preheat oven to 180°C/160°C fan-assisted. Grease two deep 22cm-round cake tins; line bases with baking parchment.
2 Beat eggs in medium bowl with electric mixer about 10 minutes or until thick and creamy. Add caster sugar, about 1 tablespoon at a time, beating until sugar is dissolved between additions. Gently fold triple-sifted flours into egg mixture. Divide cake mixture evenly between prepared tins.
3 Bake cakes about 25 minutes. Turn cakes top-side up onto wire racks to cool.
4 Meanwhile, dissolve coffee powder in the water in small heatproof bowl. Stir in marsala and liqueur; cool.
5 Beat cream and icing sugar in small bowl with electric mixer until soft peaks form; transfer to large bowl. Stir in mascarpone and ½ cup of the coffee mixture.
6 Split cooled cakes in half. Centre half of one cake on serving plate; brush with a quarter of the remaining coffee mixture then spread with about 1 cup of mascarpone cream. Repeat layering until last cake half is covered with mascarpone cream. Spread remaining mascarpone cream around side of cake; press almonds into side and top of cake. Refrigerate until ready to serve.

prep and cook time 55 minutes (plus cooling time)
serves 12

TIRAMISU LITERALLY TRANSLATED MEANS 'PICK-ME-UP', AND WE HAVE LITTLE DOUBT THAT THIS LUSCIOUSLY RICH, CAKEY VERSION WILL DO JUST THAT. CARAMELISED ALMONDS ARE WHOLE ALMONDS THAT HAVE BEEN COATED IN A TOFFEE MIXTURE

Glossary

ALMONDS
caramelised toffee-coated almonds.
flaked paper-thin slices.
ground also known as almond meal; nuts are powdered to a coarse flour texture.
slivered cut lengthways.
APPLE CONCENTRATE apple juice with most of the liquid extracted. Can be bought from health food stores.

BAKING POWDER a raising agent containing starch, but mostly cream of tartar and bicarbonate of soda in the proportions of 1 teaspoon cream of tartar to ½ teaspoon bicarbonate of soda. This is equal to 2 teaspoons baking powder.
BASIL An aromatic herb; there are many types, but the most commonly used is sweet basil.
BICARBONATE OF SODA also called baking soda.
BUTTERMILK fresh low-fat milk cultured to give a slightly sour, tangy taste; low-fat yogurt or milk can be substituted.

CARDAMOM can be bought in pod, seed or ground form. Has a distinctive, aromatic, sweetly rich flavour.
CAYENNE PEPPER thin-fleshed, long, very-hot red chilli; usually purchased dried and ground.
CHEESE
cheddar the most common cow's milk cheese; should be aged and hard.
cream a soft cow-milk cheese with a fat content ranging from 14 per cent to 33 per cent.
mascarpone a cultured cream product made in much the same way as yogurt. It's whitish to creamy yellow in colour, with a soft, creamy texture.
parmesan a sharp-tasting, dry, hard cheese, made from skimmed or semi-skimmed milk and aged for at least a year.

CHIVES related to the onion and leek, with subtle onion flavour.
CHOCOLATE
chips hold their shape in baking.
dark eating made of cocoa liquor, cocoa butter and sugar.
hazelnut spread we use Nutella. It was originally developed when chocolate was hard to source during World War II; hazelnuts were added to extend the chocolate supply.
milk eating most popular eating chocolate, mild and very sweet; similar in make-up to dark, but with the addition of milk solids.
white eating contains no cocoa solids, deriving its sweet flavour from cocoa butter. White chocolate is very sensitive to heat.
CINNAMON dried inner bark of the shoots of the cinnamon tree. Available as a stick or ground.
COCOA POWDER also known as unsweetened cocoa; cocoa beans that have been fermented, roasted, shelled, ground into powder then cleared of most of the fat content.
COCONUT
desiccated unsweetened and concentrated, dried finely shredded.
flaked dried flaked coconut flesh.
shredded thin strips of dried coconut.
COFFEE-FLAVOURED LIQUEUR we use either Kahlua or Tia Maria coffee-flavoured liqueur.
COINTREAU orange-flavoured liqueur.
CORNFLOUR also known as cornstarch; used as a thickening agent in cooking.
CREAM
soured a thick commercially-cultured soured cream. Minimum fat content 35 per cent.
whipping a cream that contains a thickener. Has a minimum fat content of 35 per cent.

DATE fruit of the date palm tree, eaten fresh or dried, on their own or in prepared dishes. About 4cm to 6cm in length, oval and plump, thin-skinned, with a honey-sweet flavour and sticky texture.
DULCE DE LECHE a caramel sauce made from milk and sugar. Can be used straight from the jar for cheesecakes, slices and tarts. Has similar qualities to sweetened condensed milk, only a thicker, caramel consistency; great to use in caramel desserts, especially banoffee pie.

FLOUR
plain all-purpose flour.
self-raising plain flour sifted with baking powder (a raising agent consisting mainly of 2 parts cream of tartar to 1 part bicarbonate of soda) in the proportion of 150g flour to 2 level teaspoons baking powder.
FOOD COLOURING vegetable-based substance available in liquid, paste or gel form.

GELATINE we used powdered gelatine; also available in sheet form known as leaf gelatine.
GINGER, GROUND also known as powdered ginger; used as a flavouring in baking but cannot be substituted for fresh ginger.
GLACÉ CHERRIES also known as candied cherries; boiled in heavy sugar syrup and then dried. Used in cakes, breads and sweets.
GLACÉ FRUIT fruit such as cherries, peaches, pineapple, orange and citron cooked in heavy sugar syrup then dried.
GOLDEN SYRUP a by-product of refined sugarcane; pure maple syrup or honey can be substituted.
GRAND MARNIER a brandy-based orange-flavoured liqueur.

HAZELNUTS, GROUND made by grinding hazelnuts to a coarse flour texture for use in baking or as a thickening agent.

MACADAMIAS native to Australia, a rich and buttery nut; store in refrigerator because of its high oil content.

MAPLE SYRUP distilled from the sap of maple trees found only in Canada and parts of North America. Maple-flavoured syrup is not an adequate substitute for the real thing.

MARSALA a fortified Italian wine produced in the region surrounding the Sicilian city of Marsala; recognisable by its intense amber colour and complex aroma. Often used in cooking, especially in sauces, risottos and desserts.

MILK
condensed a canned milk product consisting of milk with more than half the water content removed and sugar added to the milk that remains.
evaporated, low-fat we used a canned milk with 1.6g fat per 100ml.
skimmed we used skimmed milk with 0.1g fat per 100ml.

MIXED PEEL candied assorted citrus peel.

MIXED SPICE a blend of ground spices usually consisting of cinnamon, allspice and nutmeg.

MUESLI also known as granola; a combination of grains (mainly oats), nuts and dried fruits.

NUTELLA chocolate hazelnut spread.
NUTMEG dried nut of an evergreen tree; available in ground form or you can grate your own with a fine grater.

OAT BRAN the hard and rather woody protective coating of oats which serves to protect the grain before it germinates.

OIL
olive mono-unsaturated; made from the pressing of tree-ripened olives. Extra virgin and virgin are the best, obtained from the first pressings of the olive, while extra light or light refers to the taste, not fat levels.
vegetable Any number of oils sourced from plants rather than animal fats.

OREGANO also known as wild marjoram; has a woody stalk with clumps of tiny, dark green leaves that have a pungent, peppery flavour and are used fresh or dried.

PAPRIKA ground dried red pepper (capsicum); available sweet, smoked or hot.

PASSIONFRUIT also known as granadilla; a small tropical fruit, native to Brazil, comprised of a tough dark-purple skin surrounding edible black sweet-sour seeds.

PECANS Native to the United States; golden-brown, buttery and rich. Good in savoury and sweet dishes; especially good in salads.

PISTACHIOS pale green, delicately flavoured nut inside hard off-white shells. To peel, soak shelled nuts in boiling water about 5 minutes; drain, then pat dry.

POLENTA a flour-like cereal made of ground corn (maize); similar to cornmeal but finer and lighter in colour; also the name of the dish made from it.

POPPY SEEDS Small, dried, bluish-grey seeds of the poppy plant. Poppy seeds have a crunchy texture and a nutty flavour. Available whole or ground in most supermarkets.

PROSCIUTTO salted-cured, air-dried (unsmoked), pressed ham; usually sold in paper-thin slices, ready to eat.

ROLLED OATS traditional Whole oat grains that have been steamed and flattened. Not the quick-cook variety. sambal oelek a salty paste made from ground chillies.

SHERRY fortified wine consumed as an aperitif or used in cooking. Sherries differ in colour and flavour; sold as fino (light, dry), amontillado (medium sweet, dark) and oloroso (full-bodied, very dark).

SUGAR
black less refined than brown sugar and containing more molasses; mostly used in Christmas cakes, black sugar is available from health food stores.
brown an extremely soft, fine granulated sugar retaining molasses for its deep colour and flavour.
caster also known as superfine or finely granulated table sugar.
demerara small-grained golden-coloured crystal sugar.
icing also known as confectioners' sugar or powdered sugar.
raw natural brown granulated sugar.

TOMATO
purée canned pur´ed tomatoes (not tomato paste). Use fresh, peeled, puréed tomatoes as a substitute, if preferred.
sun-dried available loose (by weight) or in packets (not packed in oil).

TREACLE thick, dark syrup not unlike molasses; a by-product of sugar refining.

VANILLA
essence obtained from vanilla beans infused in alcohol and water.
extract obtained from vanilla beans infused in water; a non-alcoholic version of essence.
pod dried long, thin pod from a tropical golden orchid grown in central and South America and Tahiti; the minuscule black seeds inside the bean are used to impart a distinctively sweet vanilla flavour.

YEAST allow 2 teaspoons (7g) dried yeast to each 15g compressed yeast if substituting.

Index

Conversion charts

measures

The cup and spoon measurements used in this book are metric: one measuring cup holds approximately 250ml; one metric tablespoon holds 20ml; one metric teaspoon holds 5ml.

All cup and spoon measurements are level. The most accurate way of measuring dry ingredients is to weigh them. When measuring liquids, use a clear glass or plastic jug with the metric markings.

We use large eggs with an average weight of 60g. This book contains recipes for dishes made with raw or lightly cooked eggs. These should be avoided by vulnerable people such as pregnant and nursing mothers, invalids, the elderly, babies and young children.

dry measures

METRIC	IMPERIAL
15g	½oz
30g	1oz
60g	2oz
90g	3oz
125g	4oz (¼lb)
155g	5oz
185g	6oz
220g	7oz
250g	8oz (½lb)
280g	9oz
315g	10oz
345g	11oz
375g	12oz (¾lb)
410g	13oz
440g	14oz
470g	15oz
500g	16oz (1lb)
750g	24oz (1½lb)
1kg	32oz (2lb)

liquid measures

METRIC	IMPERIAL
30ml	1 fluid oz
60ml	2 fluid oz
100ml	3 fluid oz
125ml	4 fluid oz
150ml	5 fluid oz (¼ pint/1 gill)
190ml	6 fluid oz
250ml	8 fluid oz
300ml	10 fluid oz (½ pint)
500ml	16 fluid oz
600ml	20 fluid oz (1 pint)
1000ml (1 litre)	1¾ pints

length measures

METRIC	IMPERIAL
3mm	⅛ in
6mm	¼in
1cm	½in
2cm	¾in
2.5cm	1in
5cm	2in
6cm	2½in
8cm	3in
10cm	4in
13cm	5in
15cm	6in
18cm	7in
20cm	8in
23cm	9in
25cm	10in
28cm	11in
30cm	12in (1ft)

oven temperatures

These oven temperatures are only a guide for conventional ovens. For fan-assisted ovens, check the manufacturer's manual.

	°C (CELSIUS)	°F (FAHRENHEIT)	GAS MARK
Very low	120	250	½
Low	150	275-300	1-2
Moderately low	160	325	3
Moderate	180	350-375	4-5
Moderately hot	200	400	6
Hot	220	425-450	7-8
Very hot	240	475	9

ACP Books are published by ACP Magazines a division of PBL Media Pty Limited

acp books

Published by ACP Books, a division of ACP Magazines Ltd, 54 Park St, Sydney; GPO Box 4088, Sydney, NSW 2001. telephone (02) 9282 8618; fax (02) 9267 9438. acpbooks@acpmagazines.com.au; www.acpbooks.com.au

Printed and bound in China

United Kingdom Distributed by Australian Consolidated Press (UK), phone (01604) 642 200; fax (01604) 642 300; books@acpuk.com

A catalogue record for this book is available from the British Library

ISBN 978-1-903777-81-7

© ACP Magazines Ltd 2010

ABN 18 053 273 546

Scanpan cookware is used in the AWW Test Kitchen.

To order books:
telephone: 01604 642 200
order online: www.acpuk.com